THOMAS LAIRD

MORE Advice from a Call Center Geek!

Rethinking Call Center Operations 2.0

E

EXPIVIA
·PRESS·

First published by Expivia Press 2019

Second edition

ISBN: 978-0-578-56663-4

Typesetting by Maggie Mahon
Proofreading by Cathy Lombardozzi
Editing by Joyce Covatto

This book was professionally typeset on Reedsy.
Find out more at reedsy.com

Contents

WHY A CALL CENTER BOOK 1

MANAGEMENT TRUST EQUATION- TRUE STORY 9

WANNA BET 14

CULTURE > EVERYTHING 21

SOCIAL MEDIA/BRANDING TO RECRUIT 27

SETTING UP A NEW CALL CENTER STRUCTURE 32

METRICS THAT MATTER 39

TRAIN ANIMALS, EDUCATE PEOPLE 43

CALL CENTER COFFEE 46

MONITOR LIVE OR RECORDED CALLS? 51

QA (QUALITY ASSURANCE) DONE THE RIGHT WAY 55

9 WAYS TO IMPROVE YOUR TEAMS COACHING 60

WEEKLY AGENT ANALYSIS 64

ENHANCING YOUR COMMUNICATION CULTURE 68

IMPROVING CALL CENTER ATTENDANCE 76

MANAGEMENT CULTIVATION 80

WHEN GOOD TIMES GO BAD 84

OH THE GAMES WE PLAY 88

MORE CALL CENTER GAMES! 94

ERQ: THINKING OF SALES IN A NEW WAY 100

INCENT YOUR ASSOCIATES 104

CHATBOTS 107

COST ANALYSIS FOR NON-FINANCE MANAGERS 110

THE DIRTY WORD...OUTSOURCING 112

ALL AROUND THE WORLD 118

THIS IS THE END   121

About the Author   124

1

WHY A CALL CENTER BOOK

Think about this customer interaction:
   A customer calls into the call center for XYZ company. The customer starts in the IVR. There is a hint of frustration that begins to build when our customer has to go through 5 prompts to get the right department. The customer is officially frustrated when the IVR does not understand her when she keeps saying "Change Bill Date" over and over. The customer is now angry as she screams "AGENT" while pressing zero 10 times as hard as she can.

After finally hearing the IVR say "You are now being transferred", our pretend customer gets a call center associate that is disinterested, non-empathetic and starts to frustrate the customer even more with his tone.

Even though the associate is not giving a great experience, he was trained on what to do with this call type so he goes through the motions and handles the customer's issue to a tee. The talk time is actually very short, and the issue was handled on the first call. Is that a great, world class call?

Using our outdated KPIs, on paper, it looks like a great call:
   The call was answered within an 80/30 SLA...Check

The call was handled within the appropriate handle time...Check
We had first call resolution on the call as well...Check
(I know what you are thinking, no there was not an NPS survey done after the call in my example, bare with me!)

THE EXPERIENCE WAS TERRIBLE FOR THE CUSTOMER! This customer most likely is headed straight to Twitter or Facebook and they won't be posting a positive review.

There are so many things that call center managers and executives do wrong, myself included. We look at dollars and cents (so we think) and not the customer's experience. We look at age-old metrics to define a world-class call center. We train on how associates should navigate a CRM and what screen to be on but do not educate on empathy, delight, and tone.

Because of this, most call center customer service experiences stink. *C'mon you know it's true!*

The majority of centers are run poorly, are not a fun place to work, provide average service at best, have high turnover and are looked at as low-paying, unenviable jobs. Why?

This is why I wrote this book. Let's try to change all that!

With all the new technologies out there that claim to give your customers a world-class experience, why do so many companies have below average NPS scores and legions of negative social media posts? In the era of social media, we are now getting a true gauge of who is offering amazing service and which companies are not, and the reason is **not** technology.

The reason goes much deeper. It goes to the culture of the organization but more to the point, it goes to the culture of the call center.

In this book, I want to make you think. I want you to change long-standing behaviors. I want you to ponder the way you have done things forever and ask, why? I want you to create something unique to your industry. My goal is to give you some of the needed tools to do so!

Customer experience is next to the corporate battlefield

WHO IS THIS BOOK FOR?

I am writing this for contact center managers looking for something different. Managers that want to create a call center culture that is unique and customer/employee centric. I am also writing this for the next generation of call center managers. The world you will see in the next 30 years will differ greatly from the call center world most of us have come from. I hope together we can prepare for this with some newer thinking.

My name is Tom Laird. I am the CEO of Expivia Interaction Marketing. We are a growing 500 seat USA BPO (call center outsourcer) in Pennsylvania. I have worked in call centers my entire life from the seat of a rep, to the IT technical side, to supervisory and management roles all the way to owning and running my own center. I have worked with a range of organizations, from Fortune 50 financial services organizations to small startup looking to outsource for the first time. I have seen a lot. Some good and some not so good. This book is a testament to all the awesome things I have seen a call center can be when run the right way.

I am not a writer by trade. I write how I talk. I hope you feel the realness and the passion I have for the contact center and the customer experience.

I will shy away from talking about what "new" technology you must have as technology is always changing and I want this book to help you no matter what technology you are using or will be using which we have not even thought up yet. Besides, we already agreed, technology does not make an excellent contact center on its own!

Before we get into this, I want to tell you a little story....

This is where I came from...

In 1985 a small call center was started by my parents with 10 employees in Erie, Pa. It was a family business where I grew up at. I was 9 years old at the time. Business was small but steady, allowing for a company with a reputation for quality to take hold. The company grew over the years, and a new 75 seat center was opened in 1990 to support an influx of new business. In those days, most of the business was dealing with outbound credit card sales for major banking institutions. When I came on board full time during college, it was 1994. We had just expanded to over 200 seats, and business was good. I started with third shift positions in our IT area learning the business from the ground up. I had to work my way up through the organization; nothing was handed to me.

The culture was that of a close-knit family. Many employees were there since the start, and the management team had been together for years by this time. This group of individuals was known to me as the closest of any of my family members, and we treated each other that way... in those days. It was a great place to work with a strong group of people.

4

2000s

As the early 2000s ticked by, the organization hit its stride. At our peak, we had over 700 employees and revenues well over 20 million dollars. Things were going very well. We had many high-profile Fortune 150 clients including many of the top financial institutions in the US, which as anyone in the BPO outsourcing business knows, only goes to the best of the best. I was 5 years into my job of running the day to day operations of the call center floor. We implemented many philosophies that I strongly believed in, and we were prospering. A management trainee program was put in place which allowed us to average over 6 years of tenure for all our middle management. Turnover was low for the call center industry due to the family-style culture we tried to foster. We tried to work with our associates and progress them up the ladder. Things were going great... until 2008.

2008

When the "Great Recession" hit, we lost over 60% of all our business due to financial organizations who were now under TARP, gutting marketing budgets. It was a difficult time. I thought that we would get through the troublesome times ahead though because of the tight-knit management team we had and all the battles we had fought and won. By this time, most of us have worked together for going on 15 years and knew each other for much longer.

That was a naive mistake made by me. This time it would be different. People scattered. It started with our IT personnel then to our Production Staff and then to Client Services and HR. It was as if a negative wave had taken hold of our team and could not be stopped. Management went looking for new jobs at the first sign of these troubled waters.

In 2010 the company was sold

This was the most difficult and eye-opening time for me. I was still working at the place I loved. The new owners stripped me of most of my authority. Being part of the past owning family meant I could not be trusted in their eyes. People I thought were my friends; people I fought side by side with for almost 20 years were now positioning themselves for a power takeover. These were the same people we fought for and did everything we could to save their jobs when the new owners came into the picture. The same people we took into our inner circle and worked with for almost two decades turned overnight. Losing years of friendship over a little money and power was something I could not fathom. Not everyone thinks as I do... Again, I was naive.

February 8, 2011

The plot was finally settled as I was driving home after work on February 8, 2011. I received a call I was being let go. After 25 years of being a part of the company, all the new management team could muster was a 1-minute phone call. They had listened to the wrong people. That's enough of that.

The reason I tell this is not to ask for sympathy but to tell you I have learned the saying; "life is 10% what happens to you and 90% how you react to it" is a factual truth.

Instead of laying down and taking a defeat I got together with some decedents of the company I was let go of. Knowing we could do a better job than most of the call center industry from all the centers we had seen and worked with, including the management team we were leaving, we started anew.

Greatest decision I ever made!

Expivia Interaction Marketing was born a couple of months later. We decided since we were not burdened with the overhead and cost of an older organization, we would do things differently. We would embrace new technologies afforded us through the cloud. We think of our philosophy as MONEYBALL for the call center. Many of those procedures we will discuss in the following chapters.

We gazed into the future and have looked to position ourselves in a place to capitalize on where we see customer interactions heading 5, 10, 15 years from now. Social media, APP Development, video technologies, chat-bot/Texting AI and world-class inbound/outbound sales and service could all be fostered to grow what we think is the NEW definition of what the contact center should be in today's market. We could reinvent ourselves, and boy did we.

In the first years of Expivia, we were honored to receive the Disrupt Erie Startup of the Year Award for Northwest Pennsylvania, and we were invited to join the NICE inContact iCVC board. The iCVC is a select group of NICE inContact customers selected to join as trusted advisors to help NICE inContact validate ideas for new products, features, and plans for future innovations.

Expivia is different. I want to show you how you can be different too.

BOOK FORMAT

The format of the book is very casual. We will start with talk about hiring culture. Culture is the differentiator and the organizations that get it right have a huge advantage.

Do you want to know how to hire the best call center sales and service associates? Want to know how to motivate and promote the right way? We will discuss, your culture is your beacon.

Next, we will talk about the education of your associates, Management Training and Quality Assurance. All the things that are the lifeblood of the center and concepts you must have in place before we talk about actual operations.

In the last part of the book, we will talk about the actual operation of the call center. How you should meet and greet associates. How you prepare for each day. Most importantly, with operations, how should we praise associates, deal with confrontation and have fun on the call center floor?

I have some other miscellaneous topics I think will interest you as well that get more into the back end running of the center. This includes doing a full cost analysis (oh yes, we will!) to looking at the cost difference of outsourcing locations around the world.

This is a fast read. Take notes... highlight this bad boy up! Let's improve your call center!

2

MANAGEMENT TRUST EQUATION-TRUE STORY

Call Center Management Trust Equation — A True Story

Call centers have a lot of working parts and a lot of people who try to keep everything running smoothly.What is the best way to manage a call center? Do you know? Let me tell you a story of how I learned what works best for me and my staff.

Let's go back to 2002. I was a young, naive, 20-something with a total "Type A" personality, who was put into a supervisory role in a call center. I became the AM Production Coordinator—which means I had progressed up the ladder until I was in charge of 15 supervisors and up to 175 associates.

It was up to me to be sure my AM shift was hitting its qualitative and quantitative goals for our clients. The AM shift had always outperformed the PM shift. Soon after taking this new position, my shift started struggling. Our numbers weren't as good, our quality scores were dropping, and our turnover rate was going up. All of this meant we were less profitable.

I was summoned to see my boss. When I got into her office, she asked what had been going on. I told her I was doing everything "right." If someone had a bad monitoring score, he/she was written up immediately. If her sales were down, she got put on a corrective action plan. There was literally no one on my floor who hadn't been talked to about what they were doing wrong.

She asked, "Do the people on your floor trust you?"

"Absolutely!" Then, she asked me to define what trust was. "Trust means you don't lie to people. You are honest and trustworthy. That's what I am doing. I am giving them honest feedback to let them know what they are doing wrong, so I can help them."

"Yes, that's part of it," she said. "It's a very small part of it." She told me she had learned something important through the years: **Trust=Character+Competence+Motivation.**

She asked me to consider what other word could be substituted for *Trust.* I was supposed to come back and tell her when I figured it out. I obsessed over this. What could it be? After much longer than I like to admit, it came to me; but, I had to start by breaking down what the words in her equation meant to us as management in the call center world.

Character

Character: that's a lot to think about. Your work character starts to grow as you come into the workplace but is honed when you come into a management role. You have to make your job your own.

It begins with making sure you are on time every day, that you are dressed appropriately, and that you show that you care about the job that you do. Character comes through in how you are viewed while you are on the floor. It's about not backstabbing people, not using bad language, and not lying to coworkers. It's about letting your team know that they can depend on you to do the right thing.

Competence

Many managers equate competence to being a person who knows more than everyone else. However, the truest form of competence is being able to make more good decisions than bad ones. It's not about knowing everything; it's about making better decisions because you can see what the outcome could be. This knowledge comes when you take time to listen to your team. Listening allows you to make suggestions alongside your team before you put together the best answers to take back to management.

> *When I first started, I felt threatened when someone else had an idea.*

If this sounds familiar, know that you are not alone, but then just listen. You really need to listen to what the people on the floor are telling you—they live and breathe this job on the front lines and often have really good ideas.

Motivation

To be trusted, you have to be motivating. Not every manager is the cheerleader type, but you still need to stay positive with your team. When you are positive, your team will feed off of your positive energy.

Negative energy is counter productive—spread lots of positivity in your call centers!

You still give corrective actions when warranted. But, you are coaching in a way that gets your point across, without the employee getting defensive. If they get upset, don't take it personally. Keep your positive attitude when you are out on the floor, show that you have the motivation to get things done in the right way for the entire team.

Trust comes from showing that you are real and want to help others succeed. Competence shows when you make good decisions that benefit both the company and the reps. Motivated people are positive and others naturally gravitate towards them.

This brings me back to the word my supervisor wanted me to figure out. When I finally had my light bulb moment, I went back to see her. I knocked on her door, poked my head inside, and said: "RESPECT."

"That's the word! THAT is management." She was right. Knowing everything, being bossy, and correcting everyone is not what gives you power. True power lies with the supervisor who is respected and trusted because they are competent in their job, have high character, and are positive and motivating.

This idea is the bedrock upon which Expivia is built. This experience from my 20s is something I use now with all of my supervisors, especially when they are having a rough time.When I see someone on the floor not performing like they should, or having issues on their team, I will ask them one question after they tell me they are "doing everything right."

Do your reps **trust** you?

Keep this in the back of your mind as we make it though the next couple chapters.

3

WANNA BET

I bet you I know why your call center is struggling!

In helping companies with call center outsourcing, we have seen many reasons call centers and customer service struggle in many organizations. I bet as you read through this section, some of these will ring true in your organizations. The first step in correcting a problem is knowing you have one. This is not meant to be an absolute list, but these tend to be the seven cardinal reasons we see why call centers struggle. We will address these (and many more) as you get deeper into the book. Take a second and circle or highlight some issues you see in your call center. This way, when you get to the chapter on fixing these, you can drill down on what is most important to you and your call center.

It's okay if you have issues in your center, that's why you downloaded this super expensive eBook... lol!

The first core reason we see centers struggle is an unneeded focus from specific organizational departments that don't understand the impact they are having on the call center and on the customer experience.

1) WHO HAS THE SAY IN YOUR CUSTOMER SERVICE CALL CENTER

Who is running your USA customer service call center? Is it your financial department, your marketing department or your sales execs? Who has the most say, who is the squeaky wheel that always seems to have to be appeased? The mindset of the people running your center has a lot to do with the culture and the personality of your center.

Now a great center can still balance all these different aspects but when one takes over as being more important, as what happens in a lot of companies, you can have a disconnect, and the customer takes the brunt. If...

FINANCIAL IMPORTANCE IS THE KEY DRIVER

When this happens, you feel the pressure of being efficient even to a fault. High service levels do not mean as much as low AHT, Wait Times, and Wrap time. You get pressure to handle more calls in a shorter period. When this happens, you have a couple issues, first; you already have irritated customers before they even get to an agent because of long wait times in queue, second; when reps feel the pressure of quicker calls the service of the call drops. This has a snowball effect as well because the bigger the queue, the more pressure you and each of your supervisors put on the reps to handle the next call!

ARGHHHHH!!

We have all been there! It's funny when you look at the SL and Wait times for people calling in to buy something from the company, those skills/queues (I will use "skills" from now on) gets overstaffed while the customer service skills for questions is understaffed.

This is true in so many companies. *COMPANIES STILL DO NOT REALIZE SELLING TO AN EXISTING CUSTOMER WHO IS HAPPY WITH THEIR SERVICE IS SO MUCH EASIER AND CHEAPER THAN GETTING NEW CUSTOMERS TO BUY FOR THE FIRST TIME!*

In these companies run this way, it's like pulling teeth to add staff yet there is little technology spend either. I am sure a lot of you can relate.

MARKETING/SALES IS YOUR KEY DRIVER

So many USA customer service centers, rightfully so, are trying to make their center not just a customer service center but a profit center. Nothing is wrong with cross-selling your customer service calls if we all understand it is an add-on.

Some mistakes we see here is when:

A) Your cross-sell effort does not match your call type (we have seen crazy things clients have tried to sell just for a quick buck)

B) Your selling effort takes over as the main reason for the call:

Then this happens not only are you not getting a sale, but you may be losing a customer. You must handle the customer's issues first; build a rapport and then try to cross-sell a product that meets the needs of the customer. Do you just keep track of how many sales your reps have in a day, probably posted in the room right? Do your top salespeople get all the rewards? I hope you have your quality scores and reps satisfaction scores posted as well... most don't.

2) EDUCATION

Most companies put all their education (Notice we said Education, not Train, you TRAIN animals, you EDUCATE people) in how to run a specific program, skill or channel, (What to look for, what screen you have to be on, what button you have to click.) They do NOT do a great job of facilitating tone and delight in their calls. Most companies want to educate as fast as they can, so they can have reps producing quickly even to the detriment of the customer. Remember you must understand that in the age of social media your customers will talk to others. We want them to be evangelists for our brand. We must understand this as we educate.

3) NO FLUID PROCESSES

Large and small companies can all have this issue, but most of the time, you see it in large companies. When multiple departments have a say in how the customer service for their specific channel is to be handled, you can get inconsistent and confusing service. Different 1-800 numbers, transferred calls, multiple call resolution. It's super frustrating! When told by a company associate, "they do not handle that issue in his/her department" the frustration level rises, and you may have already lost that customer. Disjointed departments all handling sales/service is a huge reason for the lack of service in the marketplace.

4) WRONG METRICS (Moneyball stuff!)

So many companies have in-house USA customer service centers stuck on metrics such as First Call Resolution, SLA, Talk Time or proprietary formulas to tell if they are good at service. These metrics *should diagnose* and put service issues and techniques under the microscope, **not be the goal**. Your goal for world-class service should be to have your customers become so loyal they become evangelists for your brand to all their friends. In the age of social media, this is the direction your company must be moving towards. NPS and speech analytic sentiment reporting are ways of accomplishing this.

5) DEPENDENCE OF SELF-SERVICE CHANNELS ONLY

Many organizations believe by FORCING self-service they are saving money by stopping calls going to a live agent. Show me a company doing this and I will show you one with low Customer Sat and Net Promoter Scores.

Just because huge companies such as Google, LinkedIn, and Facebook go this route does not make it right for you. When you get a monopoly on a specific service like those big boys do, it's another story. You are competing with many other companies, and your service will be a HUGE factor in a customer doing business with you. I will say though that just because they can do it still doesn't mean they should do it.

Self-service is a powerful tool when done the right way. It is a needed channel; it's just not done correctly. Too many organizations frustrate customers by forcing you into a long, painful IVR, or even worse; they HIDE their 1-800 numbers. YOU WANT TO TALK TO YOUR CUSTOMERS!!! You have limited chances to build loyalty with your customers... don't push them away!

6) POOR CALL CENTER CULTURE

If your customer service call center is a miserable place to work, then how can you expect great service from its associates?

The contact center can be a place where you can do things you cannot do in any other department. You can yell out loud, high five, cheer each other up! You can't do that in accounting! **Show me a quiet contact**

center floor, and I will show you one with high turnover, low quality and more importantly, one that reflects associates are not enjoying themselves.

It does not matter if you are running a center with an insurance, banking, pure customer care or sales vertical. You can, and in my opinion, *must make the environment enjoyable.*

7) POOR MANAGEMENT TRAINING

How do you educate the supervision in your USA customer service center? Do you have an education plan at all or do you just take long-tenured associates and make them supervisors/team leads when a supervisor leaves with minimal education? If you hire a supervisor off the street what education do you give them?

Most call center organizations I have seen do not do a good job in preparing their supervision for the job at hand. Many call center managers assume because an associate did a tremendous job on the phones they will be a good supervisor. Big mistake.

We have found having a solid management trainee program not only educates your future managers on their job but also shows career progression to all employees limiting turnover.

Customer service is as much an art as it is a science. Many impressive companies do a fabulous job with this. Unfortunately, there are also too many companies not understanding the impact of what poor service has on the company.

In the coming chapter, we will look at how to fix these problems with solutions maybe you have not thought about yet. I bet you want to know how to hire AMAZING call center associates huh... well, turn the page... let's go!

4

CULTURE > EVERYTHING

No one likes to talk about culture because it is so hard to define, right?

Let's take this in small pieces starting with the individual you are hiring. The beginning point of any call center culture begins with people, so it seems like the logical first step. So, raise your hand (seriously, raise your hand) if you or your HR team look at a resume, ask a few questions, maybe has the candidate take a little personality test, and off this data, you decide... oh, this person is a "fit." The first question you need to ask is FIT FOR WHAT? What do they need to fit in to... again can you describe your culture?

Your culture is how you operate, it's how you treat people, and how they treat people, it's what is accepted and what is not and how you get that across. It's the people you are allowing into your world and how they are to operate. Once it's well defined it starts to be something all your employees self-monitor. It's amazing to see when you get full buy-in on your culture.

Anyone can glance at a resume, see experience in the same job and hire. Just basing your hiring on that is a HUGE mistake especially in a call center environment where there are close quarters, and the job can be difficult. Personalities can clash, and customers will pay the price for mistakes. It is more important to have the RIGHT person that fits your company than the so-called BEST person. I know that sounds crazy, but we have found it to be true.

It's abstract when talked about but tangible in action.

I hear you through the Internet thinking *"Ok, Tom, that's all well and good... now will you please tell me how to hire awesome reps! "*

Our Hiring Culture

Through the 25 years of running a contact center, we have tried many methods of trying to figure out what methods and what traits we look for when hiring customer service associates for our center. Through all the years of trial and error, of trying everything from personality tests, job test and different interview tactics, we believe we have found what we think is the best method/system for getting the best associates in our contact center.

The culture of our company and our hiring is that we want associates with a *"Sunshine Attitude and an Entrepreneurial Mindset."* This statement is the glue that holds our company together and what we believe is a huge advantage for us. This boils down to "attitude and effort".

We know exactly the individual that fits our standard and creates the working environments where our employees enjoy each other (for the most part... lol) and come to work because they have the attitude we are looking for. It also means we have a competitive atmosphere where many of our associates want to be the best and want to move up in the company. Every employee we hire, no matter if they have 10 years of experience or no experience, must meet this standard. We believe this standard is more important than experience.

This is true for call center associates, management, programmers all the way up any C-level executive we would hire. This is also how we incent and promote.

REFINE YOUR HIRING PROCESS

Do you and your HR team look at some resumes, ask a few questions, do an interview, administer a test, and decide from this if that person is a "fit"? For most organizations, a fit is simply someone who can do the job. That is not what you should be looking for.

You need to look for someone who is the right person for your organization, not just the best call center rep. To get that, look at what's important to you. You must define your culture.

We try to pull a personality out of potential hires, such as by asking them odd questions like, "If you were a Crayon, what color would you be?" We've worked hard to come up with a list of about 25-30 questions that get at if someone has the right culture for us. Experience does not matter to us. If our training and education are good enough, we should be able to help you get where you need to be if you bring an awesome attitude and give maximum effort.

Takes Patience

You can never stop interviewing once you target a specific type of individual. That's the hard part. It takes a consistent effort to bring people in to interview. It becomes more difficult to hire quickly because you limit the pool of who you allow into your company's world. Is that a bad thing???

One benefit of this though is you have the right people in your organization. Referrals and word of mouth become a great tool for you because your employees will talk. We have found over 50% of our new hires are referrals from our employees. You've heard of the saying; you are the sum of the five closest people you hang around with? Well if we have done a great job of hiring in the first place then bringing in the same types of individuals is a no-brainer for us!

We believe in hiring the right way, you must know who you are. You are not hiring people to do a job. Anyone can do that. You must hire to continue to grow your culture. Every day we try to add people with Sunshine Attitudes and Entrepreneurial mindsets.... Our favorite kind of people!

I am sure you will find that our interview process is unique for a call center environment. We have taken a lot of pride in developing techniques to see if our standard of attitude and effort are ingrained in the candidate. That my friends I will not give out (unless you want to pay me to consult... lol). That's part of the fun of running a call center . You get to bring on the people you think will fit your company.

INCENT OFF OF YOUR CULTURE

While sales goals and KPIs are important, it's also important to make sure everything you do adds to your culture. To incent our reps, we have what we call "proficiency pay". This does not mean commission, or hitting your service level, or getting a certain amount of sale. We look at the things that are important to us: attitude and effort.

Number one is attendance. Clearly, you can't show attitude and effort if you're not here. So every week, our employees have to work 100% of their schedule. If they don't, they're not up for proficiency pay.

It is also based a small amount on KPIs, likes sales and service programs, and hitting those numbers.

We also use speech analytics to score our reps based on their sentiment: positive or negative. Reps know that if they're in a bad mood, their scores will show it. This is a great way to incent attitude.

Next we score on engagement. We do a weekly agent analysis with all our associates, talk to them, and find out if they're into getting positive feedback, training, and education. They must be giving that effort. People who fit our culture and don't give that effort don't last long. Those who do, get recognized for it with proficiency pay.

Be sure you're incenting the right things for your associates, otherwise you may be sending them mixed signals about your company culture.

ENGAGING YOUR ASSOCIATES

Your call center has leaders. Treat them like gold. If they are always very helpful, people respect them, listen to them, they're leaders, make sure you talk to them weekly. Have a relationship with them and get their opinion and buy-in to your company culture. Others will follow.

Make your employees feel involved by considering their suggestions. We use a suggestion AKA Culture Board where we have a dry erase board that any one can add a suggestion to if it enhances our company culture. Once a month we vote on which ones we want to implement. We create a committee to implement the changes and help employees feel more involved and come to care about your company culture on a personal level.

TIME TO THINK!

What is the culture of your organization right now? Is it healthy? Do people enjoy the culture or is it miserable? What is wrong with your culture? Is it a nice place to work or is there no discipline at all? Are you looking for individuals or team players? Are you more service or sales oriented?

Take a minute to write down all the things you can think of that describes the current center. Then write down how you would like your ideal, world-class center to operate. Next, slowly but surely get more of your lead people on board. Generate a different hiring profile based on the culture you deemed ideal. Implement policies that express that culture. Most importantly hold people accountable to those standards. (more on that later!)

5

SOCIAL MEDIA/BRANDING TO RECRUIT

Many call centers struggle with bringing in the right agents, managers and supervisors to work for them. It can be difficult to hire the right people who truly understand and value your services, and mesh with the company culture you are trying to create.

Many companies choose to write a simple job description and post it on their company website or Indeed. They pick a few applications and conduct interviews, choosing whomever has the most experience. Unfortunately, this method will often result in failure, as it sets up your company for low-quality service and eventual disaster.

FIND YOUR CULTURE

Going all the way back to earlier blog posts, we discussed call center culture. It's important to define the culture of your call center. It can be distinct from the culture of your company as a whole. Sit down with your team and really define the kind of person you're looking to hire. You're not simply looking for a worker, you're looking for a person. What kind of person do you want them to be? How will they fit into your company's culture?

Here at Expivia, we have a culture of attitude and effort, "A sunshine attitude with an entrepreneurial mindset". We place less emphasis on experience, instead focusing on a potential employee's attitude, and that they are willing to put forth the effort to be an incredible call center agent.

Instead of conducting a traditional interview with the normal questions, really talk to the actual person. Ask them to describe themselves. Dive into their personality. Learn their values. Doing this, you can learn what kind of worker they will be.

MANAGE YOUR BRAND

To attract the right candidates, you also need to manage your call center's brand. If you are an internal contact center within a larger business, create your own Facebook page. This way, you can create a distinct brand and community for your call center, separating it from the company as a whole. In this way, a potential employee can learn about your call center culture and values from your Facebook page, as well as learn about any fun activities or initiatives your call center provides.

It's not all just about Facebook, though. It's important to maximize all your social channels. This includes Facebook, Instagram, and LinkedIn. You can create inclusiveness and excitement within your company by engaging with your employees and potential employees. Do fun things like raffles, contests, and activities, to create engagement and personalize your call center culture.

Remember, it's not enough to simply have these social media channels. You have to use them. Being active is the only way to create engagement. Respond to messages quickly, preferably by assigning an agent to keep it open on their monitor or go to an agent's phone. This shows that you care about potential employees and customers.

RECRUITING

The first method of recruiting employees is going to be your call center's website. Your website is your landing page for your entire call center. It's likely the first place prospective employees will go. Be sure to have a section of your website advertising any open jobs. Try not to just call it something generic like "Hiring" or "Employment". These terms are dry and clinical. Call it something like "Talent" to differentiate from other companies and create a sense of worth for employees.

Apart from your company website, social media is also going to be a great channel for recruiting new employees. Be sure to create engagement on your call center's Facebook page, as well as running ads. A Facebook ad campaign can be incredibly effective, as well as cost-effective. A great thing about recruiting with Facebook is that you can specify in an ad campaign which area of a city or state you want to focus on the most, all to bring in potential hires from a specific area.

LINKEDIN

LinkedIn is also a great social media channel for bringing in new blood. You can use it to recruit for middle management and programmer positions, somewhat higher up positions. LinkedIn is a great recruitment tool.

JOB BOARDS

Job boards are another great tool for recruitment. Indeed is the largest in the US, but Glassdoor and Monster are two more great options. Indeed actually is free up to a certain amount of resumes but it can bring in lower qualified applicants, but a higher amount of people to choose from. You may find your diamond in the rough on Indeed.

Glassdoor is unique in that current employees can post anonymously and review your organization as an employee. Your company's Glassdoor site needs to be managed. It's important to keep your current employees engaged on Glassdoor and posting about how positive their experience working for your company has been. You can also create an enhanced profile for your company, allowing you to tailor your company's image and profile.

Consider allying with organizations in your city, such as veteran groups or New Americans. Take a look at trade schools or ethnic organizations who can bring new languages to your call center. Create ties with these groups to source agents who have special skills. Form a genuine bond with them and create a mutually beneficial partnership, so if they have someone who they think may be a good fit for you, they'll reach out to you.

USING REFERRALS THE RIGHT WAY

Another source of recruits will be referrals. Create a referral campaign in your call center and create incentives for employees to refer new agents to you. If you have awesome employees who understand and match your company culture, this may be a great way to bring in new blood who have an equal passion and understanding of your company culture. If you are having a culture issue and there are some bad apples you are weeding out, don't run a referral campaign quite yet.

One thing we have found as we've explored recruiting methods, is that newspaper ads simply don't work. The return on investment from taking out newspaper ads or digital ads on the paper website just is not worth the investment. That's why we've developed this more streamlined approach of knowing our culture and focusing on social media. Always be evaluating your recruiting methods to see what works and what you may need to tweak or phase out. When you bring in new recruits, consider giving them a short survey asking them where they heard about the job opening or where they first learned about your company. Doing this, you can learn where to invest your time and energy.

IN CLOSING

Using these tried and true methods that have worked for us, you can recruit quality employees. By defining your culture and creating engaging social media, it's an incredibly effective and easy to recruit new blood who match your company's culture and will drive your company forward.

6

SETTING UP A NEW CALL CENTER STRUCTURE

The Stations

We have 503 cubicles; that includes the supervisor stations that are at the end of our rows. The stations that we use are a combination of 3' D X 4' W call center booths. We also use s-shaped stations that are a little bit wider. We use those for programs that require two monitors. About 80% of the stations are the 3' X 4's and 20% are the s-shaped call center stations.

NAMING THE CALL CENTER COMPUTERS

A couple of tips on the naming convention: *Don't get cute.*

Call the station something that is easy to recognize. We have three call center rooms. The Main, West and East call centers.

We've tried to get cute and name them after famous streets like Bourbon

Street and Penny Lane for our different aisles and we also named the computers that way but it just got too confusing so I don't suggest that method.

Be a little more technical when it comes to the name of your call center stations. We name the computer that is to be put on our network and then we also put the inContact, or if you're using a cloud provider you have what's called the station ID or some type of identifier for your Cloud telephony platform. We put that number on there too and when each agent logs in they know what station they are in and the station ID when they have to put that into their inContact. We use a label maker and stick it onto the top right-hand corner of the computer.

BUYING COMPUTERS FOR YOUR CALL CENTER

If you're buying brand new computers, you're making a vastly horrible financial decision.

We purchase all of our computers online through a couple of different sites. Email me if you want the name of some of the companies.

We will not pay more than $400 for a computer. Most of the computers are between the $300- $350 range and they are refurbished Windows 10 professional computers. They have one terabyte of memory and are super-fast work machines. We normally use all-in-ones, so 90% of our computers are 23-inch all-in-one Lenovo's. They are what we have found to be the hardest-working machines.

You don't need a lot of memory. We're not housing things on the actual computers. We're really just connecting to the internet and making sure that we have a good and fast computer for our reps to work on.

CALL CENTER OPERATIONS

We have a supervisor ratio of about 16:1. That's the average for some of our programs, but it can be as low as 10:1.

Each of the Reps will have the same supervisor every single day and they will also sit in the same station every day. It doesn't mean that they own the station because we have multiple shifts. So somebody that's working a 9 to 3 shift will use a single station every day and then someone working 3 to 11 will use the same station every day. They might share that station, and we want them to at least be sitting in their same home every single day or as close to that as possible with the same supervisor who knows them.

The previous podcast on how we set goals and how we talk to each of the reps every morning, is really important because it discusses how to build the relationship between the supervisor and the Associates on their team.

STATION PROTOCOL

When it comes to hanging things in the booth, we have a little bit of an issue with that. We provide our reps picture plates where they can place pictures of their family. We try to be as paperless as possible and with some of our clients, we're totally paperless so there can be absolutely nothing including those pictures in the station.

It's a security concern that we think is important. If anything needs to be hung, we laminate it and give it a policy number to make sure it can never be taken out. This may seem to be a little bit of paranoia but we're dealing with clients and we can't make mistakes. We do everything we possibly can to curb any type of issues that may arise.

WHITE NOISE IN YOUR CALL CENTER

We also use white noise in one of our centers. I go back and forth on this and depending on how you have it set up, it can be helpful. Sometimes to me it can be annoying but the reps seem to like it especially in some of the louder areas.

HEADSETS FOR YOUR CALL CENTER

You don't need to spend a ton on headsets to get really good ones. We've tried out probably five or six different types of headsets. The ones that we use you can find on Amazon for $23. They're noise canceling headsets and they last for about a year before they need to be replaced, which I think is pretty good.

CALL CENTER STAFF STRUCTURE

So we've discussed our supervisor ratio being 16:1. The training area which we call our Incubation Room is where our reps are trained before they come out onto the floor. That can be as low as 5:1 in that training aspect, then the reps go to the floor where they are introduced to their team.

From a QA standpoint, we double the ratio between the supervisor to QA. So if we're at a 15:1 ratio for the supervisor we normally do a 30:1 ratio with our QA staff. Again, that's client dependent on what we're contractually obligated to from a monitoring standpoint. We've found that we can be at that number because of speech analytics. We try to rotate the QA staff onto different programs that they are trained on so they aren't listening to the same people and getting bored.

We also like to rotate our management trainees throughout the QA area as well. They need to understand the scoring aspect of QA and what to listen for. In our 16:1, we have at least one team lead who's been there for a while or a management trainee.

On the floor, the supervisor has a 16:1 ratio. They will have about 15 reps and then one management trainee or one team lead to help them or give each other a break. It also helps them get into the groove of being a management person. We've done a whole management trainee podcast as well.

MISCELLANEOUS

Let's talk about some of the physical things in the room like TV's. We have 50" flat screens that are dispersed throughout the room. We initially tried to disperse them by one TV per team but that can be a little bit difficult with the number of clients that have come on board.

On the TV's we place the stats of the people and programs that are around that TV, post company news, and any games that we are playing. Another little tip I would suggest is if you're not sure how to utilize the TV's, look into Intel Compute Sticks. We use them on all of our TVs. They are a 4-inch computer that basically has an HDMI plug. They're Windows 10 and if you get a wireless mouse and a wireless keyboard, you can actually control the TV from another location. There are absolutely no wires and it's super slick and super cool.

I actually bring them when we have a client visit or when I'm giving any type of pitch to a new client. When I fly out to LA, I just bring my compute stick and plug it into the back of their TV. It provides me with a really cool wireless setup that I think makes a good first impression from a technology standpoint. So that's something to check out as well.

THE IMPORTANCE OF NO CELL PHONES AND SECURITY

We have a no cell phone policy implemented on our call center floor. A lot of the centers that I've been to do not have that policy, especially the internal call center guys, but it can be done. Make sure that you set up some areas off the call center floor where they can use their cell phone. But we have a policy that if a cell phone is seen or heard on the floor, it's an automatic suspension.

It goes back to the security aspects of who we're dealing with. If we have financial services clients, and we must be PCI compliant. We've been able to train our staff on this policy and it's become a cultural thing to where they understand not to bring it on the floor.

In regards to the cell phone policy, I'm sure you have concerns that you'll get too much push back and that people will quit. You won't and they won't. We feel it's really important especially because of the type of calls that they may be taking. In the early days, we made this policy decision, and it has served the center well.

PAYROLL AND BILLING

The other question I get asked a lot is, "How do we pay our reps?" or "What mechanism do we use to pay them?"

We utilize TSheets, which I think is a pretty cool Quicken product. With TSheets, we have iPads set up in a kiosk which gives us a little bit more control. The kiosks are set up all throughout the call center and reps can punch-in and punch-out on them. It's pretty cool because it has facial recognition and if the system does not recognize the person punching in or out, then HR will receive an email asking for verification. This makes it so we don't have other people punching in for others, which obviously could be a problem.

We also do all of our billing off of it too, so let's say you're an internal call center and you want to track customer service calls or sales calls to tier 1, tier 2, or tier 3 types of calls and the amount of time that each rep is on the call. Obviously, you can do that from your telephony platform but many times it gets confusing when you're paying people from different tiers. For example, someone logged in at tier-1 who gets paid a certain rate logs off and then logs into tier 3 that has a different pay rate. This system allows us to change the different projects for different rates of pay and for different clients we bill.

CONCLUSION

So that's a snapshot of how we have our room set up and how we operate on day to day from a physical structure. Also, make sure your rows are wide enough. Make sure that people aren't bumping into each other. Make sure that the chairs that you give your reps are comfortable.

One of the biggest follies that we've seen is that you may be getting chairs for a good deal, but they're super uncomfortable and the reps revolt. Have a committee for office furniture and accessories whether it's headsets, chairs or a new mouse. Make sure that the reps have the buy-in because that'll save you from a lot of pain if you order them and they hate it. It's something that I have definitely gone through and it is not fun.

7

METRICS THAT MATTER

In 2011 one of my favorite movies was released.

The movie was called "Moneyball" and it was based on the story of the 2002 Oakland Athletics MLB team and how General Manager Billy Beane thought there had to be a different way of building a team. Until that time every team based the players they wanted on subjective opinions of scouts that got it wrong a lot! Billy Beane looked hard at the math of the game. He looked at what statistics were actually important and made some real breakthroughs in how the game is played to this day.

The call center is a lot like this. Old time thinking that gives us results that continue to provide a low customer experience. There has to be a better way, right?

Let's take some time and talk about customer service metrics with a real impact on our customers, novel idea huh?

So many companies confuse KPIs and call center metrics in a constant struggle to quantify a world-class customer experience. They seem to be changing what is important......this month is AHT, next month it's SLA = VOC... all trying to justify a great customer experience.

Why are we measuring the wrong things!

The companies that measure this way are ignoring the two main groups that decide a great experience, the customer and the associate (includes processes, CRM), and put all the time and money into the measurements in between them. This makes little sense to me.

Getting away from metric scoring and looking at the process of Net Promoter Scoring is what I believe, the real first step in enhancing what you view as great service. Net Promoter programs are not traditional customer satisfaction programs, and simply measuring your NPS does not lead to success. Companies must follow an associated discipline to drive improvements in customer loyalty and enable profitable growth.

WOW! A program that does not just depend on First Call Resolution, SLA, Average Talk Time or hold times to tell a company they are offering great service. As we have been saying for many years, these metrics should diagnose and put service issues and techniques under the microscope, not be the goal.

Net Promoter Scoring programs basically ask one simple question and work from there— How likely is it that your customer would recommend your company or product to a friend or colleague? I know you ask this question at the end of every interaction, right? You think you have an NPS program in place then right? ... nope, not at all.

What I am here to stress today is that:

"WORKING TO GET YOUR NPS SCORE IS NOT AS IMPORTANT AS EMBRACING THE PROCESS!"

Embrace the Net Promoter Scoring Process... How? Remember, the goal is to get your customers to recommend you. Let's look at some basic recommendations that would include:

- Look at the whole call process. Are there wait times, annoying IVR prompts, bad self-service processes?
- Are you utilizing multi-channel/Omni-Channel (voice, email, chat, self-service APPS/IVRs, Chatbots, social CRM and now VIDEO) interactions with your customers?
- Are your associates trained not just on how to navigate screens but on treating your customers like family? Delight, empathy, not fake "I'm so sorry" but true engagement with a customer? Too many service centers just assume associates will do this even though they are trained poorly.
- Is your call center the "fun" place to work in your company or is it the "corrective action" place? Show me a quiet call center, and I will show you one with poor quality and high turnover.
- Do you have an organized monitoring platform that provides instant feedback? Do you educate poor calls and CELEBRATE great calls or do you punish the poor calls and ignore the good ones?
- Are you using metrics such as FCR and SLA's as the measure of great service? If you are, it's time to realize they are a tool and a tool only.
- Stop the annoying wait "infomercial" and belittling self-service "tips" that we think will lessen calls to the Center and costs through your IVR. Embrace the chance to talk to a customer. Don't waste the opportunity by being petty.
- Are your middle management supervisors properly trained or are you just pulling well deserving associates and giving them the keys with no training?
- Most importantly, BE DIFFERENT. Since when did the standard for service become bad self-service, infomercial wait messages, and reps that are not into it...but hey service level is 82%. How does that make any sense?

Now listen, I am not anti-metric. I just believe they should diagnose and drill down on issues in your call center. They should not be how to determine what call centers rock.

Net Promoter Scoring and more importantly the Net Promoter culture make your company develop a culture of service which is more important than any metric and it is measurable. In the era of social media your customers can be your greatest ally or your biggest headache. So, don't just look at numbers and metrics; develop a culture where your customers become your evangelists and their loyalty grants you more customers.

Let's celebrate the proper things. Utilize the Customer Service metrics that enhance the customer experience of today.

8

TRAIN ANIMALS, EDUCATE PEOPLE

How are you educating your new associates? Do you have a specific onboarding plan for them?

Most call center turnover happens in the first 90 days of hiring. When this time is not handled properly, the organization spins its wheels in having to hire and train more, and the employee has a miserable experience. A no win situation. Let's fix that.

1) Initial Training

One HUGE mistake is starting program training too early in the new hire process. The first 30 hours of training should be spent on instilling culture (We talk about attitude and effort all the time!), getting to know the associate, talking about the company as it relates to policies and procedures. We also talk about legal call center stuff such as DNC, TCPA and recording laws. We want the associate to understand we know what we are talking about and have them understand who we are and what is to be expected.

We also educate on tone. We drill the tone. If you really think about it, the tone of the call is 90% of the message. If your associate's tone is off, then it doesn't really matter what words are being communicated as the customer is going to tune you out and become defensive. The tone is huge! We drill into each associate that the:

"TONE IS THE MESSAGE!"

We fix any lingo or "street" language. Our standard is a world-class center. We make sure before we start program training the actual program that the associates buy into that. If they can't, then we part ways at this point before we get too deeply into the process.

If you start program training right away, you are not getting to know the new hires, and you will get the culture they will impart, not what you demand.

2) Program Training

Most of our clients have extended training windows for 4-6 weeks. That's a long time. You must make sure you are having fun in the training room. The atmosphere needs to be light, and you need a trainer that understands the culture you are trying to instill. Make sure you are not just teaching your associates which buttons to press and where to press it but are actively talking about tone and engagement. You must keep drilling tone, delight, engagement.

When we role play, AKA Scrimmage (I'm a sports guy), we focus more on how things are said than anything else.

The last step is to create tests that must be passed at 100% before they can move to live calls.

3) Incubation

When new associates go on the phones for the first time, we move them to a room right off the floor, what we call, the Incubation Center. Here we have a controlled environment that has a supervisor ratio of no more than 8:1 although it's much less if you include the training staff. They are heavily monitored and coached. Once we feel they are competent enough to join a team, (the timing is different depending on the individual), then and only then will they have to join the regular team on the main floor. We will never let someone out on the floor that we do not think can be at the standard we demand.

4) Graduation

We believe in ceremonies, certificates, balloons and high fives for awesome accomplishments. Passing through training and going to your permanent team is an awesome accomplishment. We sit the newer associates with the management trainee (our team leads... remember), and they are now a full-fledged associate that will receive a raise in pay.

DON'T RUSH EDUCATION. When you do, it's bad for your bottom line, employees and most importantly your culture.

9

CALL CENTER COFFEE

Starting the day the right way!

Controlling an associate's first 30 minutes is the number one operational tip I can give. If you get nothing out of this entire book, I hope you implement some daily shift starting procedure. It will INSTANTLY improve your call center.

Our Supervisors know it is their responsibility to control the first 30 minutes of an agent's day. I originally got this idea from Dan Coen in his book, "Building Call Center Culture" but have evolved the original idea a bit.

IT BETTER BE LOUD! (Relative to culture for you lame call center managers)

First thing is that the call center room needs to be a dynamic place! The call center should be loud, music can be playing at the beginning of the shift. If music is not your culture, then find what would be the equivalent.

Your supervisors must have energy and be very positive, and you should be out there leading. Maybe you have balloons or special charts/pictures up. Whatever you do, do not have a dull, boring room. Electricity must be pulsing through the room, especially in the morning.

WELCOME WITH ENTHUSIASM

I can't stress how important this is.

All associates should be greeted as they come to their teams by their supervisor.

They need to get welcomed with a handshake and a SMILE with a GOOD MORNING/AFTERNOON. Maybe you are a high fiver like I am, don't be afraid to dole those out if that's your personality!

Honestly, I am not joking here, I really mean greeted! Not some lame head nod or a quiet "hi Jane" but a "WHAT'S UP JANE!", "How was the birthday party over the weekend!".

I understand that in an outbound world, that can be much easier to do as they have standard start and stop time for the most part. Inbound can be a little more difficult as you will have reps that come and go all day depending on how their schedule is made, which is normally based on volume. IT MAKES NO DIFFERENCE!!! Your associates are important; they must be treated as such.

I like a little personal talk here as well (So Jane how was Austin's birthday over the weekend). This is the time when we can see who is in a great mood and ready to work and who we need to work on to get in a good mood (humor works well here, more on that later). You cannot be a good supervisor and be blind to personalities and moods. Doing this as your associates come in shows that your supervisors care about their team members and hopefully is one small way to help respect to be given to your supervisors as well.

TAKE THE TEMP AND RECAP

Now that we have greeted our associates and understand the daily mood we can get on with the day. Daily team recaps are a MUST. Each of your supervisors should know the KPIs that their team must hit. They should recap yesterday's production, any great monitoring/goal performances. Keep everything positive here. If you must talk about a lackluster day, that's fine but do not do it in an angry or disappointed manner. Remember that was yesterday and you don't want that same vibe to attach itself to today.

Individual rep recaps should be done here as well focusing on yesterday in a one on one setting. Talk about the individual goals given out yesterday, where they did well and where the opportunities for improvement are. We also will need to be giving out individual goals for the present day to each rep. This is a 30-60 second talk with each rep that should be done at some point during the first half hour. Some of my supervisors like to hand out post-it notes with an individual's goal on it so they could look and focus on it during the day.

(A quick note on individual goals) Whether your KPIs run the range of just being quality based or hard nose sales-based goals, each should be assigned to the skill level and personal plan (see the previous blog) that matches each rep. Every center has a few stars, mostly average employees, and a few laggards. You can't make a goal for someone who is struggling equal to the stars on your team. If you make everyone's goals the same, you will frustrate certain employees who are struggling, and you will see a higher turnover. Stars are not born, they are created. Some will get there quicker than others but know your reps.

Now we have greeted our reps, recapped the day from yesterday on the team and individual level, and now have daily goals for the team. We have focused our team on what we need for them to accomplish.

I like to make sure that two more things are talked about to each rep during the first 30 minutes as well. The first one being...

ENJOY YOUR JOB

HOW ARE WE GOING TO HAVE FUN TODAY!

Each supervisor on my production floor must have a game or competition going at all times. This is not the same as a weeklong or month-long motivation to give away baseball tickets to the room for the top performer or highest quality score. This is something that each team likes to do, and the personalities on the team dictate these motivations. These are just little things we can do during the day to make work fun.

Little things such as the top rep for the hour gets to sit in the supervisor's comfy chair. Have bingo cards that are made up of KPIs. We have a whole section coming up on games that can be played in the call center that cost nothing - yes, I said nothing! Your supervisors have awesome ideas for this as well. Keep a library for all your supervisors to use. Our library is up to over 125 games all from my supervisors!

49

WORK TRANSITION

The last topic for the first half hour is going over any issues/topics related to the program(s) they will be running. I like to do this last and right before they take their first call of the day, so it is fresh in their minds. Our company has an intranet program called "Coaching Briefs". This is updated all the time with program information. Things like "Yesterday a mailing went out for XYZ bank that was sent accidentally so expect calls on..." This way we all know what was going on and how to deal with the situation.

As you can see, We place a huge responsibility on supervision to be PREPARED and to be ready for a shift....so should you!

10

MONITOR LIVE OR RECORDED CALLS?

There is a minor debate in the call center and quality management circles on whether it is best to use live calls or recorded calls when evaluating call center associates. We have many clients that have differing views on this as well. We have been using both models for many years and layer them on top of one another to create an overarching QA plan that takes into account the associate and program health.

Being a high school basketball coach, my work team sometimes gets annoyed at me for using sports references time and time again, but I think in this case it will really help make sense of what we do when evaluating live calls compared to recorded calls.

Live Calls help you **Win the Game Today**
   Recorded Calls help you **Have a Great Season**
   Bottom line...You need both

CALL CENTER MONITORING USING LIVE CALLS

Live monitoring from your supervisors and/or your QA areas is like in-game coaching. You are looking to make the adjustments to win the game at the moment. If an associate is not using a proper greeting, disclosure, upsell or close we need to fix that right away. Many times, we all will look at certain stats or metrics like real-time SLA, AHT, Conversion or Sales data; we look to see who is out of the norm, listen to them and make "game time" corrections to help get back to the winning score. (AKA getting the KPI's where they need to be!).

Live monitoring, in my opinion, must be done to correct issues on the fly and make sure the day stays on track. Now if we are seeing trends or issues with the tone in certain reps, we are certainly going to look to address this but for the most part, we use live monitoring to make sure we are doing what we should, hitting the proper KPI's and surpassing quality metrics.

One of the AWESOME tools that has come along to help us has been advanced speech analytics. We now can "listen" to every call that comes into our center and judge the agent sentiment (positive, neutral or negative) and then hop on the line if we see any negative or neutral trends from our agents. It has allowed us to really drill down more "in-game" to make any quick technique corrections. In my opinion, it is the best QA tool to come out in years.

While being an in-game coach is important, we also must review past "game film" to correct trends. This is where listening to recorded calls comes into play...

CALL CENTER MONITORING USING RECORDED CALLS

When you are evaluating and scoring recorded calls a different mindset should be taking place with your monitoring team. This is where everyone should be getting evaluated not just the associates outside of specific KPI's like the real-time monitoring seems to be focused on.

While live monitoring should be focused on winning the day, recorded calls should be listened to, with the thought of raising the overall quality of the program. Adding them to your training and making sure any customer trends are being noticed (if you are not using analytics).

It's like when I watch film after a game, I don't care about the score nor do I look at what adjustments need to be made during the game. I am looking at the bigger picture of what we can do to be better for the long term, our next 10-15 games'.

Every client we have, we give one hour of non-billed weekly education. We use the recorded calls as great tools in these training sessions. We find trends, scripting issues, bad or good rebuttals to use, all things that help with the overall health of the program. These help all the associates succeed.

I think you get a feel for your team when you take a step back with recorded calls. Do you need to work on the tone of the team, are there things we need to retrain? Score the call, score the individual but after that think about the program as a whole from what you are hearing.

We are still pulling associates here with any issues we find or just as importantly any GREAT calls we find as well. But as a rule, we use the recorded calls more for big-picture issues that an associate or a program may be having.

Using both live and recorded calls in your call center monitoring gives you the optimum opportunity to create the best call center team possible!

11

QA (QUALITY ASSURANCE) DONE THE RIGHT WAY

Most companies focus all their education on how to run a specific program, skill or channel. What to look for, what screen do you have to be on, which button do you have to click. They do NOT do a great job in facilitating tone and delight, empathy and engagement in their calls. Most companies want to educate as fast as they can so they can have reps producing quickly even to the detriment of their client or customer. Remember you need to understand in the age of social media, your customers will talk to others. We want them to be evangelists for our brand. We must understand that as we train.

If you truly want to have a world-class center, this model needs to be flipped on its head.

Before I talk about measuring quality in your center, there are some amazing tools that we utilize at Expivia that you may want to look into yourself when it comes to benchmarking quality.

In our center, we use advanced speech analytics that trend customer conversations. We also can pull agent sentiment reports to see who really is creating a great customer experience. Advanced speech analytics allows us to basically listen to EVERY call that comes in, not just the small percentage that get scored. It has revolutionized the industry.

Most companies do not have this technology (at the time of publishing). This will help those looking for a cost-effective way to enhance customer experience. The only thing this will cost you is the time it will take to implement.

This chapter is for the smaller call center that either has no QA area at this time or has rudimentary processes. This really will show you how to start your first QA monitoring area from the ground up.

"THE TONE IS THE MESSAGE" Remember that?

Delight for me is that certain element that makes great customer service representatives. It's the tone in the voice that wants to give quality; it's an actual thought process as to truly wanting to assist that customer as if it was a family member they are helping; it's a quality call flow process that meets a customer's needs.

The great associates can tell a customer "NO" and still be thanked. Most are not born with this skill, but it can become part of how they approach their mindset.

The first thing you need to attack when looking to change the quality of your calls would be to listen to as many associates/calls as you can. Make no changes, just listen. It is okay if you become frustrated. Remember this is the stuff we must fix.

So many call center managers don't monitor, and many others do not know what they should be hearing. You want to get a good feel for the different types of calls that you take and how your associates respond to these calls. This would include meeting with all call center middle management as well to get feedback, and to get them on board to understand how we will raise our quality standards.

CALL BREAK DOWN

What you need then to get started after you understand the calls, is to break down each vertical by call flow. You would also want to know what the main goals are to focus on. Where are you weak, where do you need to focus on the quality effort? Is it overall rep satisfaction, one call resolution, length of call satisfaction, or other things of this nature?

Let's say for example we are having many associate complaints, so we neet to get our associate satisfaction scores up. I suggest you break down the call into segments and find out where you are having most of your complaints.

For Example:
  · Opening/Greeting
  · Verification
  · Issue handling
  · Resolving stage
  · Call to action
  · Upsell/cross-sell
  · Close

EDUCATE WITH A PURPOSE

You would then come up with an education plan to train these areas separately from a DELIGHT standpoint. How are we greeting customers, are there specific words to use during the verification, how is our tone when we resolve their issue, are we empathetic to their need no matter if it was our fault or not, do we know of lag times during calls where we

MUST make small talk? Small talk is huge in engaging your customers if done well. How do we form a relationship quickly with each call? All these segments must be educated so the rep understands how the customer should be treated during each segment.

Even if your calls are more free-flowing, you can always break them down to emphasize certain elements.

If you have major issues with quality and delight, I suggest being more specific with what an associate can say (more scripted) and make them focus solely on their tone. The better they get with the tone, the more freedom they get to go off script.

DON'T BE TONE DEAF

An associate tone is the number 1 factor (IMO) to a high-quality call center. We have talked about this but it cannot be stressed enough.

The next step would be to come up with a QA monitoring form to score all calls this way. You then do weekly benchmarking sessions to make sure your team understands the scoring method and are all on the same page. Your form should break down the segments and score each one from a delight factor. I like a 1-5 scoring, but it doesn't matter if you score and you are benchmarked.

INSTANT FEEDBACK PLEASE

The last step will make a huge difference. You must make sure that you or your monitoring team is giving instant feedback to the supervisors and associates. All scored calls must be sent directly to the floor from QA right after the call is scored, do not wait! Develop a simple rule as well to make sure that all reps are heard in a certain period of time. Any rep that fails the minimal level of satisfaction on a call must be pulled immediately and retrained on the specific areas where they have issues. This needs to be done in a positive way. They are also re-monitored within a *half an hour of going back on the phones. That is very important.*

I am not a fan of recording calls then a day or two later talking to the associate. Instant feedback provides the greatest benefit. It's a lot more work, but it is very worth it. Don't be lazy.

POST QUALITY

If quality is to be improved, then you should post daily and weekly quality ranking in the center. You can do daily team and weekly center motivations around this topic.

If you have a Net Promoter Score program (which is highly recommended) make sure your associates understand it and have it posted for their viewing.

This is the first thing that I would do in coming to a new center with quality issues. There are many other things we can do to help with quality, but this gets right to the heart of how you can educate your associates and "fix" your center.

12

9 WAYS TO IMPROVE YOUR TEAMS COACHING

It can be difficult to turn the information you glean from monitoring into actionable goals to help improve your call center reps. Today, we'll be going over different ways to improve the coaching in your call center and turn these statistics into actionable improvements. There is no one way to do things and you'll of course add your own spin on these items based on the culture of your call center.

1. UNDERSTAND WHEN TO COACH OFF THE FLOOR

If someone achieves a perfect score on a quality assurance test, make sure everyone knows. Celebrate that achievement. Give your other reps reason to strive. It's always best to keep things positive.

If you must do some sort of coaching that is not positive, do it off the floor. Don't give your reps negative feedback on the floor. Pull them aside to a private conference area to give them feedback.

2. BE SPECIFIC

Always be sure to be specific when giving feedback to your reps. Your reps may get agitated and start leading you down a verbal rabbit hole, causing you to be unable to fully explain what you mean. Be ultra-specific when you're giving negative feedback especially. Give thorough details. If you give them room to argue, you may not have an answer for them, and it will make you look weak and undermine your authority.

3. THE TONE IS THE MESSAGE

Do not be negative. Don't start your coaching session on a negative tone. Your reps will immediately get defensive. They will automatically try to defend themselves, and whatever you say next, they will not take as an improvement goal. Start off the conversation positively. Try the sandwiching method. Deliver negative feedback between positive feedback. Reinforce the good things.

4. TIE GOALS

Tie your reps' performance to goals. Each of your reps should have an individualized goal. In your coaching sessions, make sure to tie the feedback to goals. Give them something to aspire toward. Give them feedback that relates to those goals, small steps they can take to help achieve them.

5. LET YOUR REPS GIVE FEEDBACK

Have your reps assess their own performance. Have as sit-down with them and let them review themselves. Instead of suggesting issues, prompt them and listen to their responses. Try to verbally steer them toward understanding their own improvement points, then you can reinforce them. Try to lead them to their own decisions that you can then reinforce.

6. ROLEPLAY

Try roleplaying the issue. It's one thing to say, but it's another to do. Try replaying the portion of the call your rep is struggling with and help them roleplay it. You be the customer. Go through what your rep should be saying and how to fix the problem. Help them practice what they should be working on and give feedback.

7. REDEFINE GOALS

Sometimes you may give a broad goal. You may need to narrow it down or redefine it. Try breaking it down into smaller, more attainable goals. Understand that not everyone will be a star from day one. Make sure the goals that you give match the expectations and skill level of the associate while still putting them on a track to meet standards.

8. UNDERSTAND EXPECTATIONS

Make sure your reps know what you expect, but also that they understand the consequences if they don't meet those expectations. If a serious mistake is made, it may be necessary to send someone home for the day. Your reps should know that is a possibility. There should be no subjectivity in responses to negative feedback. Make sure everyone knows ahead of time your progressive discipline policies.

9. RE-MONITOR

Every time you coach someone, within the next 30 minutes – 1 hour, score them again on the areas which needed improvement. Someone other than the first person who coached the rep the first time should listen the second time. Listen to live calls so you can correct any issues as soon as they pop up. Recorded calls are important, but live calls are important to keep the customer experience from falling.

CONCLUSION

Using these techniques, you can coax the best performance out of your reps. By coaching your reps in a positive way, you will increase the customer experience and create a better atmosphere in your call center.

13

WEEKLY AGENT ANALYSIS

Call Center Quality management and education must be a cornerstone of any contact center. Do all your contact center/customer service agents have a current, up to date improvement plan? Do they understand their goals for quality, sales, conversion or net promotion? A lot of centers just do a quick morning meeting and then get on with their day. If that is the basis for your rep's improvement/goal setting, then let's look at something easy to do that I think can benefit all centers.

You would never go on a long road trip with no kind of map or GPS, right? How can your associates and supervisor know where you want them to go unless they too look at their map for success? We call this our *Agent Analysis program... your map to success for your agents.*

Having a basic Agent Analysis program should be one of the corner-stones of developing high-quality representatives. It not only shows that you care about the standards set, but it also shows reps you care about them; it shows you care about their personal development. They can see there is a path to career progression.

Each of our associates is pulled from the floor for at least 15 – 20 minutes a week... ***Tom did you say 15-20 minutes a week!!!! Off the phones!!! With a Supervisor too!! No Way could we do that in our center...***

My response is, how can you afford not to! This is the most powerful culture and training tool we have. It is a total investment into our people. So in short... *figure it out... lol*

In these meetings the manager/supervisor talks a little deeper about how they are doing, what they must do and how they can help them. The tone of this meeting must be primarily positive in tone. You cannot have your reps dreading their 15-minute Agent Analysis meeting every week; it makes things counterproductive.

1) Review

Talk about the past week, what were the quality/sales/conversion goals given last week to that rep. Did they meet the goal? If not, then talk about how they can better achieve these goals in the next week. Your supervisors must be prepared for this. They must give specific examples to help the reps. ("Janie we talked last week about recognizing closing signals in your calls, I think you have done a little better especially yesterday when you... ") Go over recorded calls here if you have any specific to the goals you set the past week. Talk about their specific monitoring scores. What's that... you say, your reps don't have monitoring scores... well, more on that later.

2) Address

Any attendance/dress code/team behaviors should be brought up at this point. This is the only part that may get a little negative, so I like to sandwich it between the recap of the week and the next week's plan. Everyone has some things they need to work on from an HR/Policy standpoint. Whether it is coming a little late to work, not being in the best mood (attitude/effort issues) or fooling around too much. This is the time to address any issues in a positive manner off the floor. This takes education for your supervisor to handle. Make sure they do this

65

right.

3) Goal Planning

Give each associate SPECIFIC individual plans/goals for the week. Make sure the given goal is attainable. Your stars will have higher goals and expectations than your newer reps, although you should be ramping up a little quicker with your new reps...

Understand as well the KPIs for the program they are running. Make sure the individual goals correspond to the program goals. I know that sounds rudimentary but so many times call centers just have overall center goals. They must be broken down to project goals.

Be specific, for example: "Janie we need 3.0/5.0 quality score average for all your monitored calls for next week. You were really close to that this week, so I know you will be able to do this. I would like to see your conversion go to 6% from 5.2% next week on your cross-sell opportunities as well. Recognize those closing signals we talked about and listened to in your monitored calls, and you will be above 6%! We also had a couple days missed last week so let's shoot for a full week; I know you can do it!!!"

4) Progression

End the meeting talking about their career plan, if possible. Do they want to be a management trainee, supervisor, team lead? Do they want to learn more programs? And yes, do they want to progress to work at a different company in a higher role. This time is not about you or your company, it's about the employee, investing in them. This will go a long way in how much trust they place in your management team when there is a culture of real caring. Talk about how you can help get them to the next level. This is very important in keeping turnover down.

Associates should feel as if your team is taking the time to help them grow and move up. Deep down in places we don't always talk about... everyone wants to be thought of in a positive light...help bring this out of your people.

5) Document

This meeting should be documented in a database or simply in email or excel. You must have this for both the supervisor and the rep but also for you and the contact center manager to look at to understand how a supervisor's team is doing on a personal level.

Take the time to invest in your contact center agents. Remember they are the voice of your brand. Invest in them so they can invest in your customers.

14

ENHANCING YOUR COMMUNICATION CULTURE

While I really don't like to talk too much specific technology in the book as it's constantly changing, I feel confident that this communications tool will be around for a while. Hopefully!! lol

HOW TO USE SLACK IN YOUR CALL CENTER

We have used Slack for about eight months at our USA call center outsourcing BPO Expivia. We did this because we wanted to evolve past email which was getting stale in our center. We also had issues with tracking and sorting information in email. Reports would get lost, others would forget to send. We wanted a better way to look at the information being passed around the call center and we wanted employees to communicate more...enter SLACK.

While we still use email for external communications, when it comes to internal communication with the call center staff such as the managers, the supervisors, and our Expivia Quality Assurance, we are fully on Slack.

We have been using it for a while now but only started with the pay subscription to Slack about the last two months. So, for the first six or seven months, we used the free version which I think for 99% of you out there, the free version is going to work fine.

Free	Standard	Plus
$0	$6.67	$12.50
	Per active user, per month billed annually	Per active user, per month billed annually
	$8 billed monthly	$15 billed monthly
CREATE A WORKSPACE	BUY STANDARD	BUY PLUS
For small teams wanting to try out Slack for an unlimited period of time.	For teams and businesses ready to make Slack the hub for their projects and communications.	For businesses that need SSO, Compliance Exports, and guaranteed uptime on a single Slack team.

You don't get full functionality, but for the majority of people who use it, they give you enough in a free version. You get 10,000 messages that will hold until it writes over them. However, in my opinion, a 10,000 message quota is a ton.

In fact, it took us over half a year to get to that point. Really the only reason, we moved to the pay version is that we have clients that are using it and they wanted to join our accounts together (which is an awesome feature!) and you have to pay to do that.

How We Use Slack for a Call Center

Now, lets dig deeper how we set up our slack channels. In the following paragraphs, you will learn about:

- What we're using it for, and
- How we're using it

First of all, you need to know that we are a USA customer service outsourcing call center. Our role is to help companies who are looking to outsource their call center. Therefore, customers are contacting us and are paying us to handle customer service on their behalf for their customers. This will be a little different the most of you.

We have our production channels set up for each different project or client we have. So basically, every single client has their own channel. For an internal call center, like most of you have, you might have a sales channel, a service channel, a Tier 1, 2, 3 and so on. But for us, every client has their own channel.

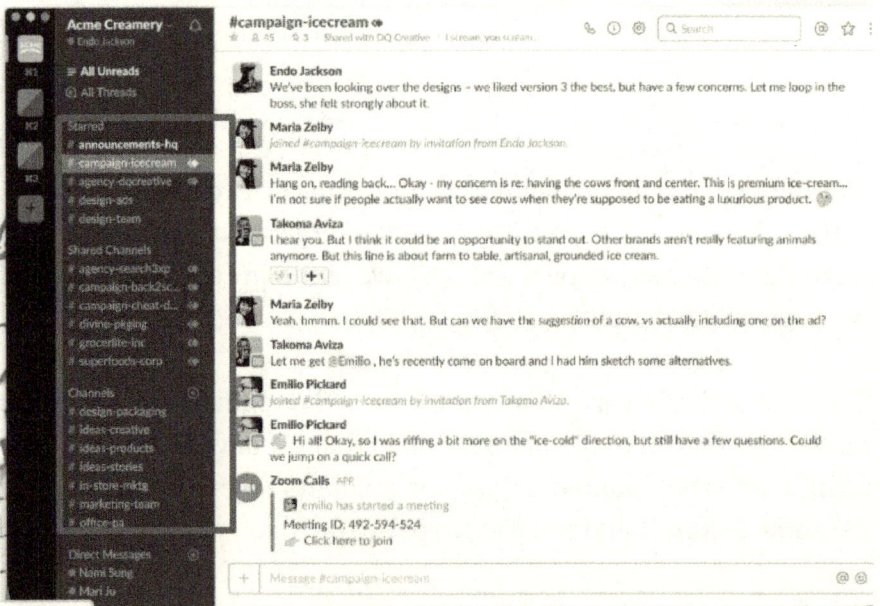

Internally, we provide access to only those that work that program or channel. This would be the supervisor, QA staff, Client Services Manager, IT manager and Sr management. We keep it tight to make sure we stay focused on what is important, and to a lesser amount for security.

Team members know that if something goes into their channel it's going to be important for them to know.

Expivia Quality Assurance Channel

Also, we have our EQA channel which is our Expivia Quality Assurance.

So, anytime that we have a monitoring issue or a rep needs pulled, we use SLACK to get that info out to the floor. We also celebrate GREAT calls in Slack as well.

Slack has really enhanced the two-way communication between QA and the floor. Supervisors may say *"hey you know Janie's been working on her tone, can you please listen to her"*, or *"we're working on some closing signals for Billy, what do you guys think."*

HR Channel

Specifically, we have staffing and HR issue channels. We do updated staffing every single day in WFM and we're making sure the supervisors know if there are any call-offs/lates for their team. Slack gets the word out to them quickly.

We are also able to send WFM reports to the Slack channel to provide a quick heads up to make sure if we need to wait 15 minutes before reps are taking their lunch today or if we need to delay a break because of staffing. Slack gets it out to the floor really fast.

If we have any rep issues (anything that is a progressive discipline issue) we're going to use the HR Issues SLACK channel. This is to make sure that HR understands what is going on in real time and they can be prepared. It also helps with our HR documentation from the supervisors.

Informal (but Useful) Use of Slack Channel

We have a YAY Channel for any type of announcement. So, if it's anyone's birthday or work anniversary, or someone had an awesome call, all that info goes in our YAY Channel. YAY is just a fun channel for cool culture things you would like to get out call center wide.

Games Channel

We keep all of our call center games in one channel under separate threads so any time that a supervisor wants to go play something, there's a repository for all that. The thread keeps all games separate so we can be adding to them all the time.

Slack Bot

The other cool thing that we've done is something we've just really started doing for the last couple of months. There's a bot that comes with Slack. This bot can basically be a kind of knowledge management repository bot (or anything you want to use it for). So, for a lot of our programs, we'll have very basic information that can be "asked" of the bot that our reps may need when on a call. Just another layer of information that can get to the floor.

celeste 4:52 PM
hey @officebot, please add espresso beans to the grocery list

officebot BOT 4:52 PM
Done! There are **4** items on the grocery list.

celeste 5:07 PM
oh! also add ice cream!

officebot BOT 5:07 PM
You got it! There are **5** items on the grocery list.

If you take just a little bit of time to set it up based on what you need, you can have information that can be pulled. Super cool feature.

Call Escalation Function

Sometimes, when the call center associates are answering calls and there is an issue that needs to be escalated to tier 2 agent or back to our client, we will use an escalation slack channel to send the information to where it needs to go. This will either go directly to our client, or to our client services manager that will pick up the phone and call the client or add it to an escalation process we have set up.

Integration with External Client

Nowadays, we've seen a lot of our clients that use Slack. Therefore, with Slack, we can actually integrate both of our accounts so that we can both access a specific private Slack channel for client communications.

So, anytime that the client wants to talk to us, or wants to send information, they can do it directly through Slack. We found that this is a really great way to do it. It allows better access to information, we can comment on it and it keeps it organized much better than in an email form.

(BTW you can integrate your email as well to populate in Slack.)

As I stated earlier, we're seeing more and more clients getting away from Skype. They are getting into Slack because it offers more functionality.

Customer Reporting

We've been actually sending reports that we normally would do via email over Slack. Again, it keeps information way more organized. Also when a client looks at them, they can comment as well in an organized thread. We will set up a thread for each report.

(FYI setting up a thread on a topic in a specific channel allows for a really clean way to deal with information. For example, let's say you have three issues in your HR channel. You can create a thread for each to keep all the data separate and apart so you don't just have a running diary of the day. It allows for specific places to put information dealing with that issue in the same channel.)

Working with Email vs Slack

You have to change the culture of how you communicate when you get into Slack.

You just have to cut the cord from e-mail because we saw that it was hard to use both at the same time. Employees stayed with what they were used to. So that's what we did. We use email only for external communication, anything internal we Slack. We have actually deleted most email accounts in the company.

I will say though if I had to do it over again, I would have made it a bigger deal in the organization to get people excited about it. We should have had more training (don't need much) and a countdown to SLACK! Something that was more fun at the time of implementation. Everyone does love it now that they are using it every day but do not underestimate the power that email had on us...lol

Finally..

All of this is really just the tip of the iceberg for what you can do with Slack. I'm not even getting into the really cool fun things about Slack. For example, how they set up emojis and GIF's for communication. It allows you to really almost express yourself when you're communicating with employees internally. You can use API's to integrate and populate Slack with your internal software and processes.

It really helped the whole culture of our organization from our attitude and effort standpoint to not only talk more to each other but to have more fun actually doing it.

I would definitely take a peek at the free version. You might not even need the paid version. Slack will evolve your communication culture beyond email. It's fun, easy to use and naturally makes your teams talk to each other more.

15

IMPROVING CALL CENTER ATTENDANCE

Good attendance is something that must be ingrained into the culture of your center. A strong attendance record is necessary for everything that we do here at Expivia. There are two main pillars of our center: Attitude and Effort. Attendance is a **HUGE** part of the "effort" pillar. We hire, incentivize and pay based on the associate's performance within the two pillars, making attendance even more important.

There are four tools we use to help our attendance, and only one of them is "negative", we believe in much more of a less stick and more carrot.

These four tools combined have helped us maximize our associates' desire to work their maximum number of hours.

CALL CENTER ATTENDANCE POLICY

All of our associates are scheduled as full-time, working 37.5 hours per week. Our goal is for every one of them to work every scheduled hour every week. Our HR policy includes 40 unpaid, personal hours per year. Unpaid personal hours carryover year after year. One associate that has been with us for 3 years, used 15 personal hours, so she has 105 hours banked. Again these are not paid, but they can be used at will for any time off needed an employee may need.

If a person goes under 37.5 hours, we will start to look at trends that might be occurring by checking their 4, 8, and 12-week averages. If they are missing more and more time, HR will meet with them and they will be placed on an improvement plan. *Not all plans are the same.* It could be for three weeks or three months—it depends on what the associate and HR agree to during their meeting. Also, it's important to note, if an employee knows she has to catch the 4:45 bus to get home, or he cannot get into the office before 9:20, they need to speak to HR—it is possible we can accommodate that. Not everything is one-size-fits-all.

ATTENDANCE FROM THE SUPERVISORY LEVEL

Supervisors are given notification of any improvement plans that are put in place. It is up to them to check in with associates during their weekly Agent Analysis chat. These chats allow supervisors to chat with the associate about their attitude, attendance, dress code, KPIs, goals, etc. Which lets the supervisor get a good feel for each individual representative.

When discussing motivation with high-attendance individuals, we may gift them with a small motivational gift to let them know we appreciate them. However, if the representative is on an improvement plan, this time is often used to really stress the need for good attendance and remind them of our incentivization practices. These associates are also meeting with HR once a week to be sure everyone is on track for success.

CALL CENTER ATTENDANCE PAY MULTIPLIERS

Attendance is important, but do you have it tied to your pay scale? We do! We use what we call *"Effort Multipliers"*. Every associate has a "Control Base Rate," which is their standard hourly pay rate. When an associate hits 100% attendance, they get a bonus of $1 per hour added to their rate. When they have done this for four weeks in a row, the bonus changes to $1.50 per hour. If they continue to have full attendance eight weeks in a row, this bumps up to a $2 per hour bonus–which is where we have the bonus capped. The multiplier amount will vary from center to center, especially depending on location.

This has proven to be a great way for us to reward our employees with high attendance. *Higher attendance levels are mutually beneficial!* We are able to bill more hours as a company, while the associates are taking more money home in their checks.

CALL CENTER ATTENDANCE PROFICIENCY PAY

We offer proficiency pay based off of our speech analytics technology for our inbound call associates. This may be a little trickier to assess if you are not using speech analytics. For us, the associates who receive a specific sentiment score will get proficiency pay. Proficiency pay is simply another multiplier that can be added to an associate's hourly pay rate. But, to be one of our proficient associates, they **must** work 100% of their scheduled hours.

For the outbound side, this is based on hitting a certain number of sales or conversion. Our outbound center is very customer-based for our client's customers. Our associates are expected to meet certain sales targets. When these targets are exceeded, proficiency pay becomes a possibility **IF** the associate is also working 100% of the scheduled hours.

The bottom line is that if you offer incentivized proficiency pay (or commission), you have to be sure to tie it to your most important KPIs, which for us is occupancy and attendance. We need as many associates here daily providing our world-class support as possible.

CALL CENTER ATTENDANCE MOTIVATIONS

Notice attendance motivations are NOT in this list. These types/motivations for great attendance can be fun but are not as important as the culture we build with the four tools above. Broader motivation is often much better for everyone than a one-off motivation. Attendance motivations have a short-term, minimal effect when you incorporate it into your culture.

Attendance is something that all call centers sometimes struggle with. When consulting, I see too many organizations that are looking to fix motivations quickly and not looking to incorporate it in their culture.

16

MANAGEMENT CULTIVATION

You can't expect your employees to exceed the expectations of your customers if you don't exceed the employees' expectations of management. " -Howard Shultz CEO Starbucks

How do you facilitate call center management education at your customer service center? Do you have a training plan at all or do you just take long-tenured associates and make them supervisors/team leads when a supervisor leaves? If you hire a supervisor off the street, what training do you give them?

Most call center organizations I have seen do not do a good job in preparing their supervision for the job at hand. Many call center managers assume because an associate did a great job on the phones they will be a good supervisor. Big mistake.

I liken it to a sports analogy. Just because you were a great football or basketball player does not guarantee that person will be a great coach. It's the same thing with your customer service center employees.

I have found having a solid management trainee program not only trains your future managers on their job but also shows career progression to all employees which limits turnover.

Management Education Program Overview

I like to have my tenured supervisors each have a management trainee on their team. That way if they must go to lunch or are sick, the team is covered. When the main supervisor is there, they are on the phones working and learning. We don't do team leads. Our team leads are our management trainees, and we like to have one per team.

Here is a rundown of the 3-6 month call center management training program. We chose 3-6 months as it's short enough where we don't lose people but long enough to mean something. This will be different for every call center so you must find what will need to be stressed for you. The outline is good though to show you how to start.

When?

I try to have a trainee class when needed. While it is fine to hire a couple of trainees off the street, I believe it is much more beneficial for the organization to try to hire from within. This way we can have classes just when we need them and do not have someone designated a management trainee for a long period and getting frustrated by there being no supervisor position available.

Weekly Management Training Meetings

We would have an hour weekly meeting where most training would take place. This is the fun part. You can tailor this to the needs of your operation. I put a ton of emphasis on leadership, how to act on the team, how to deal with tough reps, dealing with confrontation and how to turn attitudes around. I want to give them all the "psychological tools" for them to succeed.

We will also train on systems (call management system, workforce management, the theory behind how and why we route calls).

I give them some printed chapters from my favorite leadership and coaching books. Techniques to get right to the heart of helping them in their job.

One of the most important classes is our legal class. We make sure to go over sexual harassment issues, what you can say and what you can't say on your team. Any company policies such as dress code are all handed here as well to make sure that all our middle management are professional and do not open us up to any litigation.

These meetings are also the times when we train how to properly start and end a work day, controlling the first 30 minutes (a whole chapter on this!), how to do weekly agent analysis and career progressions, and how to make their reps evangelists for your brand.

Make these meetings important and special. Give special binders out so trainees can put their takeaway somewhere. Have some water/Soda and maybe some snacks. Make it something your employees want to attend. Also, be prepared for these meetings. I have a lesson plan I make to cover all the topics I want to be conveyed over the weeks of the training. I would love to tell you exactly what to teach here, but it will depend on your business type. If you would like more information on what I do, please contact me.

On Job Experience

If you have the time, it's great to have each trainee spend a week or two in all the company's different departments as well to see how everything works together. They can see when errors happen how it affects the company and how each department depends on another.

Remember as they are learning this, they are applying it every day when their main supervisor is on break or lunch. We also sit in on trainees while they are doing supervisor weekly agent analysis reviews and any monitoring issues that arise with associates.

Final Test

Once you have them educated on all aspects of what it means to be a supervisor in your organization, it's now time for the final test.

They are given a team (8-10 associates) for one week on their own where they are reviewed. Make sure they are closely supervised but given enough responsibility over that team. Give each supervisor specific KPIs for their team but most importantly watch how they are interacting with the associates.

Graduation

If they pass and you feel they are ready, then it's GRADUATION TIME!!!

We have a small swearing-in ceremony before a shift (normally on a Friday) where they would take an oath (let me know if you want the oath), get a diploma and then have balloons and cake. We also present them with a new name badge as well. Make it fun. They put a lot of time in, they deserve a little recognition.

There are a lot of different ways to cultivate culture in your organization but none more important than having your middle management buy into it.

17

WHEN GOOD TIMES GO BAD

Managing Confrontation on the Call Center Floor

Confrontation in the workplace will happen. How we manage it is a trained skill that all managers must have. These are some tactics that we cover in our management trainee program here at Expivia when talking about call center confrontation strategies. These can be easily transferred to any manager who leads a team.

Every contact center deals with people. Some come to work in good moods, and unfortunately, some do not. To make sure that your customers are being serviced in the right way, we should make sure our middle management is armed with the tools to handle an associate having a difficult day and seems confrontational. Sometimes these situations may turn into the worst-case scenario of having some sort of argument on the call center floor. These little spats will happen. Arming your management with the tools to deal with them as they happen is very important in developing a great working and customer care culture.

There are many ways to handle confrontation between supervisors and associates in a call center environment. We want to give you five basic ways that supervisors can limit difficult situations on their teams.

1) SUPERVISOR RESPECT

The supervisor must be respected. This is not something that is just given; it must be earned. If you are not arming your supervisors with the tools they need to succeed, then whose fault is it when there are issues in the center? If there is a lack of supervisor respect, then you will have unneeded situations arise. They must be the first one to show up on the team, dress the right way, have the most amount of program knowledge, and most importantly, have a want to help each team member succeed... In short, they must be great leaders. You need to put the most amount of your day constantly working with your middle management team. If they are world-class, the sky is the limit. If they are average, how can we expect our reps to be more than that?

Ask yourself, have I done all I can to make stars out of my middle management?

2) UNDERSTANDING OF EXPECTATIONS AND CONSEQUENCES

Make sure everyone knows what is tolerated, and what is not tolerated in writing. You can give a quick quiz on dress code, attendance issues, how to address management and things of this nature in their initial training. Having a company handbook online for each associate to look at and know what is expected, and if those expectations are not met, what the consequences will be...is a must-have.

There is nothing worse than having HR, your supervisors, or yourself act as judge and jury when it comes to inappropriate behavior. When you leave consequences to be dealt with in a subjective way, more issues arise. If these things are in writing, the consequences are known and are not up in the air depending on who is handing them out.

3) DON'T LET THE SITUATION LINGER

If there is an issue on a team, the supervisor must take care of it immediately, and they must do this off the floor. If an associate has a blowup on a supervisor, then we take both off the floor and deal with the situation. If you are not sure who was at "fault" then what I suggest is you send your associate home for the day after getting a statement from them and tell them that the incident is under investigation.

If it was a little blow-up, then we document the incident and hopefully move on after both are talked to. We are talking though about bigger issues that happen on a team. SOOOOO many bad mistakes get made on spur of the moment judgments. Take a deep breath, get an associate statement, and send the associate home. Then get a supervisor statement. Because with how well we believe my supervisors are trained, we normally have their back unless they admit they were wrong (which is OK!!!) and we deal with it from there. We try to call the associate and have them come in for their shift the next day for a quick meeting if we think the situation has calmed down. If it's a big deal and the associate was wrong, we will tell them of their consequences over the phone (1-3 day suspension... or whatever your penalties are).

4) KNOW YOUR ASSOCIATES

If every supervisor takes the time to know their associates on a professional level, then a lot of this can be avoided. Supervisors must know what motivates certain individuals. Humor for Suzie, Rah Rahs for Janie and tough love for Jeff are all tools that your supervisors must be trained on and know how to deploy. Also, know the strengths and weaknesses of each team member individually.

5) MANAGE PEERS

Meaning do they understand how to handle relationships with those they do not have authority over. This gets overlooked so much but we must watch and train the proper way for supervisors to handle those that they do not have " authority" over. How do they handle business relationships with peers, those above them and with those in other departments? Do they handle these with respect and understand the positive example they are setting for their associates or are they handling these improperly which will make it much harder for them to manage their team?

This is not talked about very much and is such an important part of managing in the contact center world where your associates are with you all the time. Trust me, they see everything their supervisor does good and bad. They can't fake these relationships.

Moral of the story:

Properly trained middle management will cut down on a ton of confrontational issues.

18

OH THE GAMES WE PLAY

Motivational Call Center Games!

Call center/customer service work is hard. Representatives on the phone can take a ton of abuse no matter what channel they are working. The environment must be one of comfort. And yes, it's okay to say... FUN!

Our job is to make the customers that interact with our center have a world-class experience. We cannot do this if our associates are lethargic, have bad attitudes and do not want to be at work. One way we can help them is by making the contact center *THE fun place to work.*

The contact center can be a place where you can do things you cannot do in any other department. You can yell out loud, high five, cheer each other on! You can't do that in accounting! **Show me a quiet contact center floor, and I will show you one with high turnover, low quality and more importantly, one** that reflects the associates are not enjoying themselves.

If we can get our associates to have fun at their job, it takes their mind off all the negative things that hamper great contact center work. All contact centers have associates that seem to always come in with their daily troubles on their sleeve. All contact centers have reps that leave "sick" every day because they are just plain bored. If we can take their attention off these things and channel it into something positive, then we have taken a huge step in improving our center.

It does not matter if you are running a center with an insurance, banking, pure customer care or sales vertical. You can, and in my opinion, *must make the environment enjoyable.*

DECOR

Look at your center. Most of you are probably at work looking at this book so take a second to look at your center... I'll wait... lol.

Does it have energy, or is it just plain and boring? If you were an associate, would you like coming to work in this room every day? For that matter, do *you like coming into the room every day!*

I'm not saying you need to overhaul your center if it's not where it should be. There are a couple of basic things you can do. Also, I would love to get some of your ideas on this as well.

Balloons can add a ton to a room. Just some "company" balloons or "great job" balloons go a long way. As basic as that sounds, if you give a balloon to each team's top producer daily based on your specific KPI, it goes a long way for morale and adds to the fun look of the center.

Team Crests/logos/mascot pictures can brighten up the room and add to a great team spirit. Just having each team decide a team logo can be a lot of fun for the team members. You can even make a game out of it where each sale/great call/cross-sell gets to add a name for consideration, and the top producer gets to pick the name. Use your imagination.

Posters. I really like to put up great sayings my reps used on a call. It's a reward for them to have a poster "named" after them and the phrase will get more use because an actual rep used it. Having generic posters in a room is okay but just gets ignored.

GAMES

I have a TON of games that can be played in a call center, enough for a whole book (hint hint!) This hopefully will give you some ideas. These are games that can be played daily on each team. Every day, each supervisor MUST have some game going on with their associates. You can do team vs. team or rep vs. rep. Please understand these are daily games to help keep our associates focused on their daily job and to have fun. These are not monthly or quarterly sales or service motivations for your overall top producer. That's a separate topic.

Bingo

Set up a board that includes some KPIs that can be measured during the day. Each time an associate hits one goal they mark it off the sheet. Once they get enough, BINGO gets yelled out, and you have a winner.

Poker

Each time a rep hits a KPI they get a card. Best poker hand wins at the end of the shift or the end of the week.

Pass The...

Like the chair, we will pass an object for each Sale or KPI hit. If it's summer, I will go get beach balls, and we will pass or hit around a beach ball, winter, maybe a stuffed Santa. You can award the owner of the ball each hour or just once at the end of the shift.

Off the Clock Sports

Reps love to be off the phones, it's human nature. Set up some games like having a putting green on the floor, little nerf basketball hoop or some darts up in your center. Again, however you have it set up, great sale, great monitoring score, KPI hit, the rep gets to get out of the booth and go play the game for a small prize. The real prize though is the 5 minutes off the phone.

Hangman

Pretty self-explanatory. Supervisor sets up a board, and the word/phrase, and the reps get rewarded with chances at guessing a letter and the word or phrase.

Human Board Game

We set up a "board" that goes around the center. We put down "lose a turn," "Go back to start", "move ahead 5 spaces" ...on the floor of the center. We then will move around playing pieces of the associate's choosing like a board game. Use your imagination. The associates are great at setting these boards up.

Battleship

Set up a board full of prizes (5-minute break, candy bar, 10 dollars) and ships that represent each team. Every time an associate hits a metric, they get to choose a space. They try to sink the other ships and get prizes.

Rollerball

Use your imagination here. We set up a garbage can on one end of the room and set up some cool ramps where the reps will roll a ball and try to get it in... Make a different setup every time!

Pyramid

Every rep that hits the KPI gets a chance to build a pyramid with red solo cups and then take it down to earn a prize... again this is off the phone time for them. Here is a link to this in our center!

Eye Spy

Supervisor sees something and every KPI a rep gets, they get a guess... good for days when you need to engage reps.

Sorry

We have set up giant games of Sorry we play. We create the games on a big dry erase board, same with Monopoly. Just rename some properties for people and places in your center.

Those are all just a small sample of games a supervisor should be playing on his/her team. Remember this is besides a center-wide motivation that maybe runs for a week or a month. Email me for more if you are interested, my contact info will be at the end of the book.

PRIZES

What should the prizes be? Well, I can tell you they need not be big to have the reps fighting over them. Candy, lottery tickets, a new pencil or pen, cup, homemade cookies, a free soda are all things that work.

It's funny, it really depends on how your supervisor sells it. I had a supervisor give away a 5-cent pencil eraser. Sounds boring right? But the way she sold it to her reps made it sound like the greatest thing ever. They died to try to win it.

It's very important that your middle management buys into this. I cannot express the need to have energetic supervision that leads the team. Look at some of my other posts on middle management training if you are interested.

I hope you enjoyed this look at some of the call center games we play; it brought back some great memories of some of the fun I have had on the call center floor. I hope it gets you to realize how important your role is in the overall "fun" culture of your center.

19

MORE CALL CENTER GAMES!

For the updated version of the Geek!, we wanted to give you 13 MORE games.

Prizes vary for each game. They can range from cash, a cup, candy, a lottery ticket, extra break time, or even going home early with pay!

Punch out

Pin 20-25 Solo cups to a corkboard, and then fill some of the cups with small prizes: lottery tickets, cash, or wrapped candy. Leave a few cups empty, but also fill some with shaving cream for laughs. Then, cover the cup with a tissue, using a rubber band to hold it in place. When a rep hits their goal, they come up to the table and pick a cup to literally punch out and keep whatever they find.

Find the Joker

Tape an entire deck of cards (with the Joker included) face down on a whiteboard. As reps hit their goals, they get to sign their name on a card. Once all cards are signed, they are pulled down one-by-one. Whoever got the Joker is that day's prize winner!

Target Practice

Reps are broken into teams. When a team member gets to play, they roll a die to see how many beanbags they get to throw. Each target gets a different point value based upon the location and difficulty level—we use a cornhole board, a Nerf basketball hoop, and a wastebasket. The first team to hit a certain number of points wins a prize such as extra break time or going home early with pay.

Horse Racing

We use the 12-inch square carpet tiles on the floor in our center as "spaces" for several games. Teams get to decorate their "horse" game piece. Supervisors create a racetrack around the call center and then each time a team member is eligible, they get to roll a die and move their horse that many squares forward. The team that gets to the finish line first wins.

Human Board Game

Before the beginning of a shift, a supervisor labels carpet tiles with different board game spaces: lose a turn, go back three spaces, swap places, roll again, etc. Each rep then creates their own game piece. They roll the die each time they hit their goal or make a sale. This game is really interactive because the reps can see where everyone else is and what they need to do to win.

Water Pong

Beer Pong at work would be frowned upon lol, so we play Water Pong instead. We draw names and pair people into a team of two; then, using a March Madness type of bracket with every team listed, matches are played at a set time. Reps love this time away from their phones to play! A tournament goes on all week. The championship round is held at end of day on Friday, when the final match is played. We play it outside when we can so everyone can gather around and cheer for their friends, without disrupting the people still working. The tournament winners get a nice prize.

Bubble Race

You may have to steal your kid's bubble mix for this one. When a rep earns the right to participate, they blow a bubble and must help it float down the carpet "track" as far as they can by blowing on it. When the bubble hits the floor, they put their team's marker down. The next person on their team starts from where they ended. All members of the team that cross the finish line first get a small prize.

Guess the Temperature

When a rep earns their turn, they guess the current outdoor temperature from the supervisor, who has just looked it up. They learn if they are too high or too low and get to guess again during their next eligible turn. That day's prize goes to the winner. Stupid yet affective...lol

Jeopardy

We set up a dry erase board as a Jeopardy board and break the reps into three teams. Supervisors have questions written out for the dollar amounts in each category. Categories relate to the program that they are running, company-related issues, company history, supervisors, or other things within their job. When one member from each team is eligible, they all go up for the question. Correct answers earn points, but wrong answers lose points for the team. This is great for reinforcing the culture you want to have in your center by gently reminding them what is expected.

Box It Up

Sometimes called Dots (or Dots and Boxes), a supervisor will put 200 or so dots on the whiteboard. As team members are eligible, they come up and draw a single straight line from one dot to a neighboring dot, with the goal being to create a box. When a team makes a box, they mark it as theirs. The winning team is the one with the most boxes.

State Bingo

If you get calls from all over the country, this is a great game. Create a table with state names in the cells. This game is played within teams (not against other teams). As each rep is on with a caller, they have to see where the caller is from and mark it on their board—increasing awareness of where all the calls come from. The first team member to get a horizontal, vertical, or diagonal Bingo wins!

Pyramid

Our reps actually practice this game because it is more talent-based than luck-based. When eligible, a rep comes to the table and gets a stack of Solo cups to create a pyramid. They must do it and then take it back down, in a given time. This is kind of like those minute-to-win-it games. When someone does it, they get a small prize—and a couple of minutes away from their phone.

Create the Mascot

Teams get a small whiteboard. As team members are eligible, they go to the board and add one feature to the mascot: the head, an eye, a hat, etc. This game really lets the creative and artistic people shine and brings about some interesting creations. At the end of the day, a manager, or someone outside of the call center, looks at each team's board and chooses the coolest daily mascot. This could also be set up as a fun Facebook poll.

We hope this inspires you to have more fun in your center! As hard as it may be, let's switch gears (That's right, time to get serious again)and start to think about how you are measuring sales in your call center...

20

ERQ: THINKING OF SALES IN A NEW WAY

We have focused mainly on a call center running mostly customer service. What if you have a sales call center? Well, I have some thoughts on this. I have always had outbound programs going on in our center. I started in this business in the mid-90s during the outbound credit card heyday on the phones.

Sales is a key component to most centers. We have thought this through as well and kind of flipped it on its head.

Call Center Sales

No matter what type of Contact Center you are operating, there is always some aspect of sales. Customer service centers are looking to upsell and cross-sell, outbound centers are looking to sell. How do you get your associates to do this the right way without having your quality drop?

Almost all internal call centers fight with the concept of interdepartmental mingling. The finance guys need the sales numbers to be X while the customer service executives need the quality to be Y. This is a constant struggle in a lot of centers. How do we meet the demand of a sales quota with keeping our service and quality metrics above board as well?

Most call centers with a sales aspect do some sort of commission, proficiency or incentive to reward sales in the center. Sometimes associates do anything they can for that sale to make a quota or sales goal leading to low-quality sales and sales that have a high cancel and low stick rate.

We at Expivia have done away with using the word "Sale" in our call center for both our inbound and outbound programs. When used, it has a negative connotation. This is a cultural aspect in our center.

We use a different term. **ERQ.**

ERQ stands for End Result of Quality. On sales programs, ERQ is the end goal. It means our associate did what the real purpose of the call was in any high-quality contact center; they secured a sale the right way. What is the "right way"?

COMPLIANCE

They fully complied with all regulations. This is program specific but includes things such as not even approaching the line with verbiage. They gave all the proper language in its full context and read disclosures verbatim. Our rule is that if you are approaching the line on a compliance issue, you are over the line.

TONE

The tone of our associate is appropriate. While sales calls and customer service calls may have different goals, the tone of the associate should be the sale. If a sales associate is pushy or talks down to customers, then they are not trained well enough to be on the program.

NO LOW COMMITMENT

They must be able to sell on the merits of the product; if they can't, then they should not be on the floor. You should never sell on low commitment either. If you are selling in the fact that the customer can cancel for a refund, then what is the point? You will have low stick rates driving up costs, and frustrating all involved, most importantly the customer.

TECHNIQUE

Their technique must be perfect. Most insurance and financial service products scripts need to be strictly adhered to as they have gone through many eyes at legal. Are they following the script? For our scripts, we teach our guys to follow the script. If a customer asks a question, you answer it leaving nothing out, they do not leave dead air for the customer to take control of the call. They must transition the end of the question back to the script.

GET THE SALE

Fifth and last on the list is did they secure an ERQ. The ERQ is a RESULT of the quality steps being done right.

Anyone can get a sale; they are easy. Anyone can fudge information. Anyone can push sales through. That takes no talent and no skill.

Getting a "sale" in our organization is looked down on. Change the culture of your sales center.

All centers with a sales aspect should not be looking for sales; they should be trying to achieve the End Result of Quality or ERQ.

Think about how you are selling right now. Do you have quality conversion or "stick" rate issues? If so, then you need higher quality sales. This is a great way to do that.

21

INCENT YOUR ASSOCIATES

One of the big questions I always get asked is, how do we incent our associates?

We as an organization have thought long and hard about how we can incent not just based on a couple of key metrics but to incent based on our culture. How do we do that? How do we motivate based on the pillars of Attitude and Effort?

Well, we came up with something called Proficiency Pay. We calculate who are the most proficient associates for each week. The reward is a boost to their hourly rate based on a scale.

What is Proficiency Pay?

While I don't want to get into the calculation we use as it will be different for every organization based on what you think is important to your culture, I will tell you the ingredients.

We based it on the two cornerstones of our culture so:

ATTITUDE:

1) Supervisors Grade

Supervisors grade this on the weekly agent analysis. We talk to reps about being in a great mood on the floor, and we score them on it.

2) Sentiment Reporting

Something we utilize is speech analytics which has helped us quantify attitude. We get real agent sentiment report from our analytics, and we rank the associates based on this. This is a real way we can project delight and engagement with customers into a number. It's awesome!

3) Adherence to policies

All policies must be adhered to for the week. Little things like break time overage, wearing your name badge at all times, no cell phones on the floor... all these are considered.

EFFORT:

1) Specific KPIs for the rep (not the program) are met. These are given in the weekly agent analysis meeting.

2) Attendance

Associates must work 100% of their schedule for the week to be eligible. If you are not here, you cannot be among the most proficient for that week.

3) No Holdbacks

Things like putting a head down in the booth, or not being in a good mood. This is talked about all the time and is part of our culture, so it makes sense we pay off it.

We believe in a more holistic way of incentivizing. We expect more from our associates than just hitting one or two specific numbers.

When you expect more from your team, you know what happens? When you have hired to your culture...they give more.

22

CHATBOTS

The topic of chatbots has rapidly become one of the most popular in the call center industry. There has recently been an explosion of chatbots. Some people believe these chatbots will be the end of the call center industry. While that is unlikely to happen, they can be used to enhance the customer experience and customer service.

Where we are now with chatbots is similar to where we were with IVR about 10-15 years ago. Many people thought IVR would revolutionize the customer experience and render call center reps obsolete.

RULE-BASED BOT

We have found that rule-based bots can handle about 80% of customer questions. They are also used for lead generation. Rule-based bots are basically virtual IVRs. They give you a menu and you hit the right buttons to go down the path you want. They have keyword recognition to help guide customers to the right destination. Using a rule-based chatbot can help take volume away from the call center by answering the majority of simple questions your customers may have.

That being said, chatbots can never replace a customer service rep. Some customers can find them annoying or frustrating and would prefer to speak to a real person. There should be an easy integration for your customer to turn the session into a live chat with a real person.

AI

The term AI is often misused. AI is a data-centric bot that can collect information and learn from your profile. If you've called before, it can retain that information from your previous customer service interactions. It then can present this data back to you to make your customer service interactions easier.

KEYWORD-CENTRIC BOT

With this bot, you simply type your query into the platform. The bot will pick up keywords from your message to know what it is you're asking.

CONTEXTUAL BOT

The contextual bot "learns" and assimilates your data, taking into consideration your previous interactions with customer service. It can prompt you and ask if you would like to do the same things you've done previously. This bot is more "conversational" than the previous two types.

SHOULD YOU USE A BOT?

You may not want or need a bot for your customer service. First, understand your customers. Understand the types of questions they typically ask your customer service representatives. If they tend to ask very in-depth, high-end questions, a chatbot won't cut it. They'll need to speak to a rep.

Nonetheless, you do need some sort of texting/chatting self-service, in your customer service. Almost everyone has a cell phone capable of using apps, and those customers want a fast and easy platform for answering quick customer service questions.

Look into what these different bots can do. They can answer simple questions, book appointments, buy products, and help you pay a bill or check a balance. These are all simple tasks a customer may not want to talk to a rep for. For customers with more difficult questions, they'll need to speak to a rep. Bots are also not quite as good at the upsell/cross-sell as a person might be.

You could even use more than one type of bot. You could have a bot to answer customer questions and another for lead generation. Before developing a bot, you'll want to analyze your data for a few weeks and narrow down your top customer questions, and if those could be integrated into the chatbot, and how.

Developing a bot can range from $10,000-$25,000 and up, depending on the sophistication of the bot. Often you may pay a flat rate of about 50 cents per use of the bot.

IN CLOSING

Chatbots provide for a very interesting technology, and new functions are being added every day. Don't panic if you haven't implemented a chatbot or if you're not sure about it. Adding a chatbot to your customer service repertoire, is something you can outsource so you don't even have to deal with the logistics, but may greatly enhance customer experience.

23

COST ANALYSIS FOR NON-FINANCE MANAGERS

Let's take a second to think about the actual costs that go into your call center.

You don't have to be an accountant to do this, but it's helpful to understand all the factors that go into the cost of running your center. There are a lot of more technical ways to do this, but one way we like to compare apples to apples is to cost out our center and divide that cost by the number of reps you have. This way you can see how much an associate is costing your organization when you add in all the support they are given.

We have a calculator you can play with on our Expivia website at www.expiviausa.com/savings-calculator. This will allow you to put in the actual numbers and see what one associate is costing your organization. It's fun to do and sometimes really eye-opening.

Here are most costs that go into an associate in the majority of call centers that you may not be thinking of in totality:
   1) Salary
   2) Payroll Taxes

3) Supervisor Costs/number of agents

4) Telephone charges

5) Equipment (Desks, computers)

6) Quality Assurance/number of agents

7) Work-Force Management/number of agents

8) CRM License

9) Training Costs

10) Rent/ Lease

11) Motivations/commissions/proficiency pay

12) IT Costs

So how we do this is to add up all the costs and divide it by the total amount of associates you have.

When you add all that in we have found on average, an associate costs roughly $59,000 a year.

Find out the exact cost of an associate at your center by going to www.expiviausa.com/savings-calculator and play with our call center calculator.

24

THE DIRTY WORD...OUTSOURCING

Call Center Outsourcing

Now that we have looked at the cost of your center in the previous, although very short chapter, please indulge me in a cheap plug for looking at outsourcing your center. In this chapter, we will look at some of the benefits of call center outsourcing.

In the next chapter, I will give you the basic pricing structure of USA, Nearshore and offshore pricing options. This is great info to have if you ever decide you need to talk to an outsourcing company. I want you to be a step ahead of the game if you never outsourced before.

If your organization cannot put in the time or the money to do a lot of the things we have talked about in the previous chapters, outsourcing to a high-end call center to do these things may be the best move for you and your customers.

There is a perception in the market you should never give up control of your customer experience to a 3rd party. The thinking is in-house facilities are ALWAYS better, right!

The fact is usually this is not the truth. From my experiences, most internal centers cannot compete with the training, technology, expertise, and cost-effectiveness of a high-end USA Contact Center BPO. Many of you sell a product or a service and "do" call center stuff on the side. This is all we do, and we are pretty good at it just like many other call centers like us out there.

When the question comes up whether to outsource or not, you must understand the difference between what your customers desire and what you can provide.

Does your current in-house center provide:
- **Multi-Channel/ Omni Channel Operations (Voice, Chat, Email, Video, Social)**
- **Fully Integrated CRM Platform**
- **Advanced Speech Analytics 100%**
- **Advanced Routing Techniques**
- **Forecasting and Workforce Optimization Software**
- **Expert Call Center Personnel**
- **Chatbot/Texting AI Capabilities Cost-Effective Operations**

If your in-house operation cannot stand with the technology of today by being at least a multi-channel facility; if you do not have the time or resources to train, monitor and track your personnel and KPIs, then you are doing your customers a disservice by NOT outsourcing.

Many customer service executives too often think outsourcing means offshoring. The issues of foreign accents handling US calls and perceived lack of quality are some of the first things, unfortunately, that come to mind. The other negative thought we hear all the time is "my program is not big enough to outsource" and "isn't it expensive to outsource to US call centers?"

These notions of outsourcing usually are just not true. There are now many cost-effective USA BPO call centers, like Expivia that offer customers more than most in-house customer service centers in quality options while still lowering costs and giving a better experience to customers than can be done in-house.

The Cost Myth

Cost can be a huge benefit when looking to outsource. The cost of telephony, servers, equipment, supervision, training, monitoring, tracking, and reporting add up. If you are not experienced at running a contact center and are just purchasing the equipment without the real knowledge, you are risking a huge expense to your bottom line and a threat to your brand and reputation.

Many think USA call center outsourcing is not a cost-effective way of outsourcing.

A wide variety of companies may want to look at outsourcing their customer service to give great service to their customers while still concentrating on their core business. This is something we at *Expivia think is especially helpful for newer businesses that want to make sure they are on equal footing with the technology offerings of larger competitors.*

What you must look at if you are thinking of outsourcing

1. Proper Size

This is the first thing a company must consider before talking to contact centers. What size BPO is right for you. If you are looking to outsource a major program 1000+ seats, then you must talk to the multi-national call centers with sites that can be as large as thousands of seats or more important have multiple sites they can place your business for more redundancy.

Most of the time though, this is not the case as many customer service programs fall into the under 100 seat range. I personally would not want my 20-100 seat program at a site with 1000 seats. In my observations, your program will fall through the cracks, and you will become frustrated. You probably want to look at a company with 500 seats or less to give your program the time it deserves.

2. Track Record of Management

What has the management team done? Are they experts in your business type? There are many niche call centers out there "specializing" in everything from financial service to IT to retail. Make sure you have a comfort level with the management of the call center, and they understand your business type.

3. Client Support Method

Client support is one of the most important points you must feel comfortable on. Some call centers, like ours, make sure you have a one-point client services manager to help you with all your needs be it production, IT, reporting, etc. Many larger call centers have clients call into the call center manager on the floor for issues. Some have you call in and put in trouble tickets! I am in the group that believes all programs deserve a center where issues can be dealt with 24/7 by a voice that understands your program.

4. Associate Match

The Call Center you choose needs to be an extension of your brand. The center you choose should match the demographics of your choice in your center.

5. Proper Technology

Have a baseline thought on what your program may need from a technical standpoint and then make sure the call center has at least that in their arsenal. Will you need call recording, virtual queues (queue callbacks), private client monitoring, speech analytics capability, chat-bots? Are they a multi-channel facility (voice, chat, email, self-service options)? Do they have onsite programmers or do they outsource programming? Can they handle any screen, CTI, and connectivity issues? The call center of today is a high-tech business. Make sure the call center you choose is up to date with current technologies.

There is no excuse not to be.

6. Onshore/Offshore/Hybrid

This is a big decision and one you must not take lightly. There are some programs that do well offshore. There are many though that need a US-based center. There are pluses and minuses here that would take a whole new post. All I will say here is you must understand your customers and the programs you need to have done. Costs obviously are much cheaper offshore, but the price you may pay in customer loyalty can make it expensive.

7. Company Culture

What is the culture of the call center? This is where site visits become important. Is the center paperless, is there energy, do the associates look like they want to be there? You cannot ask agents to go over and above for your customers if the center is not doing that for their agents. How are the agents paid, what incentives are there, what is the agent turnover, how are supervisors and management chosen? These are all important questions to get a feel for the company. Ask yourself, do they value what we do. That question must be answered as a yes, or you need to move on.

8. Training

How are their new associates on board, what training do they receive before they start on the floor? What is the ongoing training like? How do they communicate with agents about program changes? How do they handle internal monitoring?

Training of agents is huge and a topic not to be forgotten.

9. Scalability/Flexibility

Some people talk about the scalability of a call center. Can they help you as you grow yet still scale back if needed? I talk more about the flexibility of a center. Do they take the time to understand your specific business cycle and needs? Some centers do a great job with this while some will set minimums. Make sure you have a comfort level here.

10. Security

Is the Center you are using PCI compliant? They better be. It is no longer just a perk to be PCI. It should be mandatory for any call center you work with . We would suggest only working with paperless companies (no paper in call center booths) with strict no cell phone policies.

I don't want this to be a sales pitch, but this is an option if you are struggling to service your customers the right way.

If your call center doesn't rock, mine does. Look at all your options.

25

ALL AROUND THE WORLD

So, let's say you want to look into outsourcing in more depth. What is call center outsourcing pricing? Will outsourcing companies charge your company to outsource your customer service or call center voice operations? That is a question that comes up a lot when talking to new clients.

Costs differ significantly depending on the quality and budget you have. USA based, Nearshore, Offshore, dedicated or shared environments... What is the best option for you and your company? The following is an overview of what you are generally looking at when it comes to BPO outsourcing costs.

1.) INBOUND VOICE SERVICE/SALES

USA/NORTH AMERICA

Dedicated

Call Centers in the USA "generally" price themselves at $23–28 an hour with the average being around $26.00. Now, this is the average for a regular customer service program. If you are looking for specific skills like tier 2 tech, licensed insurance agents, registered nurses then these per hour costs are normally in the $30 – $50 per hour range with some going much higher if the skill is hard to find.

Per Minute

Per minute charges for programs rage from $.52 – $.70 cents per minute but again can go as high as $.90/minute for specialized programs (licensed agents).

Most call centers use an occupancy of 75%. This means associates are in a billable state 45 minutes out of every hour. If you take $.52 * 45 minutes = $23.40. That is how you get the per hour charge.

NEARSHORE

Nearshore Inbound/Customer Service ranges from $12 – $17 depending on the country you are looking to outsource to. Mexico is low to mid-teen/hour.

OFFSHORE

This is a little bit of a wildcard with all the countries and different large and small BPOs operating in the space. You can pay as low as $4 – $6 dollars an hour for centers in India and Pakistan, but the going rate is normally between $7 – $10 dollars an hour.

2) Outbound Call Center Outsourcing

While there are many pricing models when it comes to outbound marketing these are the rough non-commission (Pay for performance) hourly rates you will find.

USA/NORTH AMERICA

USA rates are from $22-$28/hour for standard outbound programs (sales, follow up, appt generation, service calls). Any advanced skill programs (licensed agent) can run from $30-$50/hour. Pricing for inbound and outbound in the states is similar, so it makes it easy to multi-skill agents in both from an efficiency standpoint.

NEARSHORE

Call centers in the Eastern part of Europe and Latin America are in the $9-$16/hour range. Again, Mexico is in the mid-teen range.

OFFSHORE

In general, you will find agencies in India and the Philippines charge from $5 – $10 per agent hour. Eastern Europe and the Middle East is a little more/hour.

I hope this gives a little more insight into how the pricing model works on a general basis.

26

THIS IS THE END

My last tip for you...

Technology is ever changing. There will be some awesome and wild tools that come out over the next years that are really going to change the landscape you and your team are going to instantly fall in love with.

Always remember these are just tools. They are the facilitators to service not of service. The call center technology of today is amazing, tomorrow will be even more fascinating, but it only works when your core culture is set and not before.

Before adding any new technology, your priorities should first be on the human interaction element. Hiring, engagement, culture, attitude, delight, proper processes, program knowledge and an overall agent dynamic based on true customer satisfaction. To sum that up...you better have well-trained agents and thought out processes or no matter what technology you have it will not save you!

If you give me the choice of a center that only offered 1800 number voice service, was properly staffed, answered calls on time, employed agents that were masters of the product and service needs, were empowered to provide a high percentage of first call resolution and educated to truly engage with customers on a positive level, you have a good chance to have world class service!

I will take that over the call center with poorly trained associates but have an omnichannel setup that allows customers to interact on their terms. This allows MORE WAYS TO PROVIDE POOR SERVICE!

The industry must start talking more about how service is done, then on how we facilitate it. Looking at LinkedIn the ratio of technology to actual call center operations and agent management posts seem like 20:1. We wonder why there are so many companies with poor service.

The true measure of world-class service is not just how you facilitate the experience...that is not service. The true measure is how your customer feels when the experience is over. Will they become evangelists for your brand or are you offering them a hollow experience dressed up with technology?

CLOSING

I hope this was helpful to you and your staff. My hope is that you will come back to this book and look at certain chapters more in-depth. I know not all of this may apply in your organization but I bet a lot of it will.

If you just take one thing from this book, I would hope you look at your culture and how you view what makes an awesome center, awesome. I hope you take a second to just make some small changes every day to generate the culture that is appropriate for your company and your customers.

Remember, it's not just looking at SLA, and AHT and CSAT scores, but looking at the entire operation. How you hire, how you educate and how you engage your reps. That's how you start down the path of a world-class call center.

But hey, what do I know...I'm just a call center geek!

About the Author

Tom Laird is the founder and CEO of award-winning Expivia Interaction Marketing Group with over 27 years of experience in all facets of contact center operations. Expivia is a USA BPO omni-channel contact center located in Pennsylvania.

Expivia is a bridge between a high-quality contact center and a high tech software company. We have integrated the latest technology (Speech Analytics, AI, WFO, Chatbots, API Integrations, Advanced Routing Techniques) with time tested education and employee engagement tactics to create what we believe is the new standard in call center outsourcing.

Tom has the honor of being a member of the NICE inContact ICVC Board. The iCVC is a select group of inContact customers selected to join as trusted advisers to help NICE inContact validate ideas for new products and features and plans for future innovations.

Prior to starting Expivia, Tom was the head of call center operations for a large BPO that specialized in financial services. Having this past know-how has given him the honor of running many services and sales programs for most of the top 15 largest financial institutions in the USA.

Tom is also the host of a weekly podcast by the same name (Advice from a Call Center Geek) and it can be found on iTunes, Spotify, Sticher, Google Play or here:

https://expiviausa.com/call-center-geek-podcast/

You can connect with me on:

- https://www.expiviausa.com
- https://twitter.com/tlaird_expivia
- https://www.facebook.com/Expivia
- https://www.linkedin.com/in/tlairdexpivia
- https://expiviausa.com/call-center-geek-podcast

Subscribe to my newsletter:

- https://expiviausa.com/category/blog

Made in the USA
Coppell, TX
24 June 2021